Women
of the
Twelfth Century

Women of the Twelfth Century

Volume One:
Eleanor of Aquitaine and Six Others

Georges Duby

Translated by Jean Birrell

Polity Press

This English translation © Polity Press and The University of Chicago Press 1997.
First published in French as *Dames du XIIe Siècle, I: Héloïse, Aliénor, Iseut et quelques autres* © Éditions Gallimard, 1995.

First published in 1997 by Polity Press in association with Blackwell Publishers Ltd.

Published with the assistance of the French Ministry of Culture.

Editorial office:
Polity Press
65 Bridge Street
Cambridge CB2 1UR, UK

Marketing and production:
Blackwell Publishers Ltd
108 Cowley Road
Oxford OX4 1JF, UK

ISBN 0-7456-1695-X
ISBN 0-7456-1947-9

A CIP catalogue record for this book is available from the British Library.

Typeset in Sabon on 11/13 pt Sabon
by CentraCet, Cambridge
Printed in Great Britain by Hartnolls Ltd, Bodmin, Cornwall

This book is printed on acid-free paper.

Contents

Introduction

T hese reflections are the first fruits of a long, risky and as yet incomplete enquiry. I have persevered because I wanted to know more about those women who, in twelfth-century France, were married to a lord, and to discover what sort of life they could lead in their world, the fashionable world, at the upper levels of that brutal yet refined society we call feudal. I have chosen to remain on these heights because only they are sufficiently well lit. But even here, much remains obscure. Historians have to struggle to make progress over a difficult terrain whose boundaries constantly recede before their eyes.

For us, the women of that distant period have neither faces nor bodies. We may imagine them, on great court occasions, dressed in gowns and mantles like those that drape the virgins and the female saints on the doorways and stained-glass windows of churches. But the actual bodies that the gowns and mantles both left exposed and swathed will always remain invisible to us. Artists, then, were no more concerned with realism than were poets. They depicted symbols and kept to conventional formulas. We cannot hope to discover the individual physiognomy of the women in the very rare portraits which have survived, though they are of the most powerful of them. No less rare are objects that they held in their hands that we can still touch. Apart from a few jewels, and those scraps of sumptuous Oriental fabrics in which we may imagine them arrayed before, given in alms, they were used to wrap the sacred relics in reliquaries, we have none of the finery they wore. We have, consequently, almost no concrete images. All our information comes from the written word.

I have started, therefore, from texts – from the few that survive from this period – and tried, at the beginning of my investigation, to piece together portraits of a few female figures. I have no illusions; it is difficult enough to form an impression of men, even the most famous of them, those who changed the world. What do we really know of the personality of Francis of Assisi, or of Philip Augustus, or even, despite Joinville, of St Louis? How much more are the women, who were spoken of far less, doomed to remain only shadowy figures, without shape, without depth and without individuality.

I should declare at the outset that what I am trying to show is not the lived reality, which is inaccessible. These are reflections, what written texts reflect. I trust what they say. Whether they tell the truth or whether they lie is not what matters to me. What matters is the image that they provide of a woman and, through her, of women in general, the image that the author of the text had formed and that he wanted to convey to his audience. In this reflection, however, the living reality is inevitably distorted, and for two reasons; first, the texts dating from this period – and this did not change in France before the end of the thirteenth century – are all official, intended for an audience, never inward looking, and second, they were written by men.

Writing, fine writing, that which has stood the test of time and that I read here, sets down only important words, and in artificial forms, either Latin or else the sophisticated language spoken at fashionable gatherings. Certainly, it was sometimes read in private – but always aloud, chewing over the words – on the benches lining a cloister, or in the chamber set aside for ladies, or in those book-lined cubbyholes where a handful of men applied themselves to copying out old sentences or composing new ones. All these texts, however, were written to be declaimed, often sung, in front of an audience. All, even those that aimed primarily to entertain – the romances, the songs and the comic tales – were intended to instruct. They did not set out to describe what was, but drew from everyday experience, freely amended, whatever could deliver a moral lesson. Affirming what ought to be known or believed, they aimed to impose a set of exemplary images. In the last analysis, the literature of the twelfth century is no more realistic than the sculpture or the painting. It describes what society wished and what it ought to be. All I can do on the basis of these words, spoken, I repeat, loudly and clearly, is to reconstruct a value system and identify within this system the place assigned to women by male power.

In this society, everything official, everything in the public domain, beginning with writing, was masculine. Historians acknowledge this in the titles they give to their books: *Mâle Moyen Age, Homo Ludens, Man and Society*. Only the men of this period are to a degree visible and they conceal the rest, especially the women. A few women are there, but represented, and symbolically, by men, most of whom were churchmen, and therefore forbidden to approach them too closely. Twelfth-century women knew how to write, and probably better than their knightly husbands and brothers. Some of them did so, and a few perhaps wrote what they thought about men, but almost no female writing survives. We have to accept that nothing of women appears except through male eyes. Yet, in essence, have things so radically changed? Yesterday, as today, society only reveals of itself what it thinks prudent to reveal. What it says, nevertheless, and perhaps, above all, what it does not say, allows us a glimpse of its structures.

I have therefore re-read texts, endeavouring to identify with those who wrote them in order to dispel the mistaken notions that have since distorted their meaning. I have attempted to forget, since I too am a man, my own idea of women, and I may not always have succeeded. To clarify the field of my research, I present here six female figures, chosen from among the least indistinct. It is a beginning and, I hope, a useful one. Another book will deal with the memory of their female forebears as it was preserved in the great noble houses; other images will then appear, hazier, but nevertheless clarifying the image of women present in the minds of the knights of that period. I propose, lastly, in a third book, to look more closely at the judgement passed on these women by the men of the Church who directed their conscience and endeavoured to rescue them from their native perversity.

1

Eleanor

Beneath the central dome of the church at Fontevraud – in the twelfth century, one of the largest and most prestigious abbeys for women in France – one sees today four recumbent statues, the remains of old funerary monuments. Three of them are carved from soft limestone: that of Henry Plantagenet, count of Anjou and Maine through his father, duke of Normandy and king of England through his mother; that of his son and successor, Richard Coeur de Lion; and that of Isabella of Angoulême, second wife of John Lackland, Richard's brother, who became king in his turn in 1199. The fourth effigy, of painted wood, represents Eleanor, heiress to the duchy of Aquitaine, wife of Henry and mother of Richard and John; she died at Fontevraud, where she had finally taken the veil, on 31 March 1204.

The body of this woman lies full length on the slab, as it had lain exposed on the bed of state during the funeral ceremony. It is wholly concealed within the folds of the gown. A wimple fits tightly round the face. The features are of a perfect purity. The eyes are closed. The hands hold an open book. Before this body and this face, the imagination is given free rein. But the effigy, admirable though it is, tells us nothing of them as they were when Eleanor was alive. She had been dead for many years when it was carved. The sculptor may never have seen the queen with his own eyes.

In fact, it hardly matters; the funerary art of this period was not concerned with likenesses. In its perfect serenity, this figure makes no pretence of reproducing what had been visible on the catafalque: the body and the face of a woman of eighty who had struggled hard against life. The artist had been instructed to show what would become of this body and face in their perfect state, on the day of resurrection. No one will ever know, consequently, how powerful were the charms with which the heiress to the duchy of Aquitaine was endowed when, in 1137, she was handed over to her first husband, Louis VII, king of France.

She was then about thirteen years old; he was sixteen. 'He burned with an ardent passion for the maid'; or so at least it was said, half a century later, by William of Newburgh, one of those English monks who were then so skilfully retelling the story of past events. 'The desire of the young Capetian', he added, 'was trapped in a fine net'; 'this was hardly surprising, so strong were the physical charms with which Eleanor was blessed'. The chronicler Lambert of Wattrelos also rated them highly. But what are these eulogies actually worth? Convention required the writers of that age to celebrate the beauty of all princesses, even the least attractive. Furthermore, Eleanor was already, in 1190, the heroine of a scandalous story which was circulating round all the courts. It was inevitable that anyone speaking of her would attribute exceptional power to the charms she had once displayed.

This is a legend that dies hard. It still today delights some authors of historical novels, and there are even serious historians whose imagination it continues to inflame and lead into error. Since the Romantic Movement, Eleanor has been by turns presented as an innocent victim of the calculating cruelty of a first husband who was inadequate and limited and of a second who was brutal and unfaithful, or as a free woman, mistress of her own body, standing up to the clergy, defying the morality of sanctimonious hypocrites and standard-bearer of a brilliant, joyful and unjustly suppressed culture, that of Occitania, against gloomy savagery and northern oppression; but, free and easy, voluptuous and a deceiver, she is always presented as driving men wild. In even

the most austere works, she appears as 'queen of the troubadours' and their accommodating inspiration. Author after
author takes at face value what the mocking Andrew the
Chaplain said of her in his *Treatise on Love*, and the absurd
sentences he concocted and ascribed to her, not least one
whose savage irony would be appreciated by every contemporary reader: 'No one can legitimately give the married
state as a reason for shirking love.' As for the games of
courtly love, Eleanor might almost have invented them. At
the very least, it was through her intermediary that these
chivalrous manners spread throughout Europe from her
native Aquitaine.

There is, in fact, some excuse for the erroneous judgements
of modern scholars. Memories of Eleanor were distorted at a
very early stage. Within fifty years of her death, the imaginary
biography of that great poet Bernard of Ventadour had made
her his mistress, and the preacher Stephen of Bourbon,
fulminating against the guilty pleasures of touch, had quoted
the perverse Eleanor as example: one day, supposedly, taking
a fancy to the hands of the elderly scholar Gilbert of la
Porrée, she had invited him to run his fingers over her thighs.
And though the tendency of that amiable storyteller, the
Minstrel of Reims, to make things up to please his audience
is well known, he was only echoing the claims of an
increasing number of people who said that the queen of
France, during the crusade, had gone so far as to give her
body to Saracens, when he ascribed to her a romance with
the most illustrious of those miscreants, Saladin. She was on
the point, he says, of going off with him, one foot already on
the boat, when her husband, Louis VII, managed to catch up
with her. So she was not only fickle, but gave her baptized
body to the infidel, betraying not only her husband, but her
God, the ultimate in debauchery.

Such fantasies were constructed in the thirteenth century
on the basis of the malicious gossip which had circulated in
her lifetime about the ageing queen. Some of it was collected
in nine of the works of history composed between 1180 and
the 1200s that have survived, and which provide almost all
we know about her. Five had English authors, since it was

then in England that good history was written. All were the work of ecclesiastics, of monks or canons, and all present Eleanor in an unfavourable light. For this, there were four reasons. The first, which was fundamental, was that she was a woman; for these men, woman was an essentially evil creature, through whom sin had entered the world, with all the confusion that was apparent. Second, the duchess of Aquitaine's grandfather was the famous William IX, traditionally regarded as the first of the troubadours, a prince who had also, in his day, titillated the imagination of the chroniclers. They had denounced the scorn he displayed for ecclesiastical morality, the laxity of his morals and his obsessive womanizing, quoting the kind of harem where, as if in parody of a nunnery, he had kept a company of beautiful girls for his pleasure. Eleanor was condemned, last and above all, for two further reasons. Twice, disregarding the submission imposed on wives by the hierarchies instituted by divine will, she had gravely sinned: first, by requesting and obtaining a divorce; second, by shaking off the tutelage of her husband and turning his sons against him.

The divorce, and immediate remarriage, scandalized the Europe of 1152. Reaching this year in his chronicle, the Cistercian monk Aubrey of Trois Fontaines recorded only the one event. Laconically, and all the more forcefully as a result, he wrote: 'Henry of England took as wife the woman whom the king of France had just got rid of . . . Louis had let her go on account of the lasciviousness of this woman, who behaved not like a queen, but more like a harlot.' Such transfers of wives from the bed of one husband to another were by no means uncommon among the high aristocracy. That this one caused such a sensation is understandable. The unity of Europe was then identified with that of Latin Christendom; the pope, who was hoping to direct and mobilize it in a crusade, was therefore anxious to keep the peace by preserving the equilibrium between states. At a time when the West was experiencing rapid growth, these states were beginning to grow in strength. This was the case with the two great rival principalities of which the king of France and the king of England were rulers. But with political structures that were still very crude, the fate of these political formations was largely dependent on successions and alliances, hence the marriage of the heir. Eleanor was heiress to a third state, smaller in scale, admittedly, but still considerable: Aquitaine, a province extending from Poitiers to Bordeaux, with designs on Toulouse. When she changed her husband, she took her rights to the duchy with her. Further, by the mid-twelfth century, the Church had completed the process of making marriage one of the seven sacraments so as to ensure it could control it. It laid down both that the conjugal tie should never be broken and, contradictorily, that it should at once be broken in case of incest, that is if it transpired that the couple were related within the seventh degree; which, among the aristocracy, they all were. This allowed the ecclesiastical authorities – in practice the pope, if the marriage involved kings – to intervene at will to bind or to loose, and so dominate the political scene.

Long after the event, the Minstrel of Reims described what determined the divorce as follows: Louis VII 'consulted all his barons as to what he should do about the queen and revealed to them how she had behaved. By our faith, said the barons, the best advice we can give you is that you let her go, because she's a devil, and if you keep her any longer, we believe she'll be the death of you. And, above all, you have no child by her'; he alleges devilry and sterility, two grave failings, and the initiative is taken by the husband.

John of Salisbury, however, eminent representative of the humanist renaissance of the twelfth century, clear-sighted and well informed, is a better witness. He wrote much earlier, in 1160, only eight years after the event. He had been with Pope Eugenius III in 1149 when the latter had received Louis VII and his wife at Frascati, Rome then being in the hands of Arnold of Brescia, another intellectual of the first rank, but an anti-establishment figure. The couple were returning from the East. The king of France, leading the second crusade, had taken Eleanor with him. After the failure of the expedition and the difficulties that ensued for the Latin states in the Holy Land, the churchmen who pondered the reasons for these reverses claimed that they resulted from this very fact. 'Prisoner of a violent passion for his wife', said William of Newburgh (and it was to explain this that he stressed the queen's physical attractions), the jealous Louis VII 'decided he ought not to leave her behind but that the queen should accompany him to the wars'. This set a bad example. 'Many nobles imitated him, and since the ladies could not manage without chambermaids', the army of Christ, which ought to have been a picture of virile chastity, was encumbered with women, hence riddled with depravity. This had made God angry.

In fact, everything went wrong on this journey. At Antioch, in March 1148, Eleanor had met Raymond, her father's brother and master of the town. Uncle and niece got on well, even too well in the eyes of her husband, who became uneasy and hastened the departure for Jerusalem. Eleanor refused to follow him. He resorted to force. William, archbishop of Tyre, though he wrote his history thirty years later, when the legend was at its height, had known the queen personally, and was also ideally placed to hear all the gossip circulating about this affair. If we are to believe his account, relations between Raymond and Eleanor had been extremely close. In order to detain the king and use his army to his own ends, the prince of Antioch had planned to deprive him of his wife 'by force or by intrigue'. She, according to William, was willing. In fact, she was 'a loose woman, who behaved imprudently, as had already been observed and as her later behaviour would confirm; contrary to royal dignity, she mocked the laws of marriage and did not respect the marriage bed'. Less bluntly expressed, this is already the accusation made by Aubrey of Trois Fontaines: Eleanor was lacking in the discretion that was proper in wives, especially the wives of kings, and which countered their natural tendency to lust.

John of Salisbury, on the other hand, highlighted only one fault, though a grave one: rebellion. Defying her husband – her master – Eleanor, at Antioch, had demanded a separation. This was obviously intolerable; it was accepted that a man might repudiate his wife, just as he got rid of an unsatisfactory servant, but the opposite was regarded as scandalous. In favour of divorce, the queen invoked the best of pretexts, consanguinity. She declared that she and her husband were related within the fourth degree, which was true, and that, steeped in sin, they could clearly no longer live together. This was a strange revelation, since this relationship, though clear as day, had never been mentioned in the eleven years they had been married. Louis, a pious man, was worried, and, 'though he loved the queen immoderately', prepared to let her go. One of his counsellors, a man Eleanor disliked and who had no love for her, persuaded him not to agree, arguing as follows: 'How shameful for the kingdom of France were it to be known that the king had let himself be deprived of his wife or that she had left him!' From Paris, Abbot Suger, Louis VII's mentor, gave the same advice: swallow your resentment, hold out and wait for the end of the journey.

The couple were still at loggerheads on their return from the Jerusalem pilgrimage, when they were received by the pope. He did his utmost to reconcile them, which was in his interests. On the one hand, he very publicly demonstrated his power to control the institution of marriage; on the other, he feared the political troubles that were likely to follow a divorce. The spouses appeared before him, and here we may follow John of Salisbury, who was present. The pope listened to their recriminations, and made peace between them. The king was delighted, still ruled by a passion that John called 'puerile', by the desire that it was one's duty to master if one was a man, a real man, and especially a king. Pope Eugenius III even went to the length of remarrying the couple, scrupulously respecting the conventions, renewing all the requisite rites, first the mutual commitment, spoken aloud and put into writing, then the solemn progress to the sumptuously appointed marriage bed, the pope here performing the role of father and ensuring that everything happened as it should. Lastly, he solemnly prohibited any future dissolution of the union or any further talk of consanguinity.

Less than three years later, it was being talked about once more, and again to justify a divorce. This was at Beaugency, near Orleans, before a large gathering of prelates. Witnesses appeared and swore, which was not in doubt, that Louis and

Eleanor were of the same blood. The marriage was therefore incestuous. Consequently, it was not a marriage. The tie did not even have to be broken, since it did not exist. No one bothered about the papal prohibition. The king had resigned himself, on the advice of his vassals, as recorded by the Minstrel of Reims, who, on this point, we may probably trust. Had Eleanor, in the meantime, gone too far? Had she behaved in a wanton manner during the visit to Paris, the previous year, of the Plantagenets, father and son? The chief reason, I believe, was that she was barren. But she was not, in fact, completely barren, and inasmuch as there was sterility, it was not on her side, as the exuberant fertility of which she gave proof in the arms of a new husband made plain. In fifteen years of marriage, however, she had produced only two daughters and then in an almost miraculous fashion. The first had been born, after a miscarriage and seven years of trying in vain, following a conversation in the basilica of St Denis. Eleanor had complained to Bernard of Clairvaux of the harshness of God, who was preventing her from giving birth. The saint had promised that she would at last become fertile if she persuaded King Louis to make peace with the count of Champagne, so ending a war which, incidentally, she herself may have instigated. The second daughter had arrived, only eighteen months before the council of Beaugency, as a result of the reconciliation at Frascati, the new wedding night and copious papal blessings. There was a pressing need, however, for the king of France to have a male heir, and Eleanor seemed hardly likely to provide him with one. She was rejected, in spite of her attractions, and in spite of Aquitaine, the rich province she had brought with her on her marriage, and which, leaving the court immediately after the annulment, she took away.

In 1152, Eleanor was once again what she had been at the age of thirteen, a magnificent catch, a great prize for whoever could win her. There was no shortage of candidates. Two were very nearly successful during the short journey which took her from Orleans to Poitiers. She managed to flee from Blois, at night, before the lord of the town, Count Thibauld, could make her his wife by force; then, warned by her

guardian angels, she avoided the road where the brother of
Henry Plantagenet lay in wait. It was into the arms of Henry
himself that she fell. Gervase of Canterbury suggests that
Eleanor had planned this; he claims that she had informed
the duke of Normandy by secret messenger that she was
available. Henry, 'tempted by the quality of this woman's
blood but even more by her lands', moved fast. On 18 May,
he married her at Poitiers, in spite of the obstacles. I refer
here neither to the difference in age (Henry was nineteen,
Eleanor twenty-nine – she had long reached what was then
regarded as middle age), nor to consanguinity, which was as
obvious and as close as in her previous marriage, but to the
suspicion of sterility which hung over the ex-queen of France
and, above all, to the prohibition regarding her issued to
Henry by his father, Geoffrey Plantagenet, seneschal of the
kingdom. Do not touch her, he had said, for two reasons:
'She is the wife of your lord, and your father has already
known her.' It was then regarded as indecent, and more
culpable than the offence of incest as conceived by the
Church, to sleep with the spouse of one's lord, whilst to
share a sexual partner with one's father was incest 'of the
second type', 'primordial', and consequently strictly forbidden in all societies. Two out of our nine historians, both
writing a little later, admittedly, and in gossipy style, Walter
Map and Gerald of Wales, report that Geoffrey had, in the
words of one of them, 'taken his share of what was in Louis'
bed'. This double testimony lends credence to the story and
confirms that Eleanor was anything but shy.

This episode had clearly given much pleasure at courtly
gatherings, and all those who envied or feared the king of
France, or who simply enjoyed a good laugh, had made fun
of him. Here is the basis of the legend, and the writers who,
in monasteries and cathedral libraries, were busy recollecting
the events of their day, enjoyed collecting such stories, when,
ten years after the council of Beaugency, Eleanor rebelled
once again, and rose up against her second husband.

She was fifty years old. No longer fertile and her charms
no doubt less dazzling, she was of no further use to her
husband. She was entering that stage in life when, in the

twelfth century, women who had survived continuous child-birth were likely to be rid of their husbands, and when, able to dispose of the dower they had received at the time of their marriage, and generally respected by their children, especially the eldest son, they wielded real power for the first time in their life, and took pleasure in it. Eleanor did not enjoy such freedom. Henry was still alive. Never still, forever galloping from one end to the other of the vast territory he had accumulated by the chance of succession, from Ireland to Quercy or from Cherbourg to the Scottish border, king of England, duke of Normandy, count of Anjou and duke of Aquitaine in Eleanor's name, he had never much cared for her. He had sometimes trailed her with him from one side of the channel to the other when it suited him to display her at his side. He had impregnated her, here and there, hurriedly. He now neglected her completely, amusing himself with other women. But he was still there.

To take advantage of what opportunities remained open to her, Eleanor was dependent on her sons, and on one in particular, Richard. The eldest, William, had died in child-hood. In 1170, harassed by the next two, who were growing up and impatiently demanding a share in power, Henry had been obliged to give in. He had associated the fifteen-year-old Henry with him on the throne. To Richard, who was thirteen, he gave his mother's inheritance, Aquitaine. Eleanor, inevitably, stood behind the adolescent boy, in the hope that, by acting in his name, she would at last become mistress of her ancestral patrimony. In the spring of 1173, she ventured further. She supported the revolt of these two insatiable boys and their younger brother. Rebellions of this type, pitting sons against a father who was slow to die, were common enough at this period, but it was rare for the mother of the troublemakers to take their side and betray her husband. Eleanor's attitude was regarded as scandalous. She seemed for the second time to be breaking the basic rules of matrimony. This was made plain to her by the archbishop of Rouen:

> The wife is guilty when she parts from her husband, when she does not faithfully respect the marriage contract . . . we all

deplore the fact that you separate from your husband in this way. This is the body becoming estranged from the body, the limb no longer serving the head, and, what goes beyond the bounds, you allow the offspring of the lord king and your own to rise up against their father . . . return to your husband, if not, in accordance with canon law, we will make you return to him.

Such a tirade could have been uttered by every lord in Europe. All were convinced, in the words of the prelate, that 'the man is the lord of the woman, that woman was taken from the man, that she is bound to the man and subject to the power of the man'.

Henry put down the uprising. In November, Eleanor was in his hands, captured when, dressed in men's clothes – another serious breach of the rules – she had been attempting to take refuge with her former husband, the king of France. Henry shut her up in the castle at Chinon. Some said that he contemplated repudiating her, on the pretext, once again, of consanguinity. This would be taking a big risk, as he knew from experience. He preferred to keep her prisoner in one fortress or another until just before his death in 1189. Throughout this period, people often spoke about her, but certainly not to honour her, as do the dreamers of today, to extol her virtues or make her the first heroine of the feminist struggle or even of Occitanian independence, but rather to denounce her wickedness. She was talked about everywhere, and the Capetian episode remembered, because her behaviour had been a vivid demonstration of the terrifying powers with which nature had endowed women, who were lustful and treacherous. It had showed how the devil used them to spread discord and sin, which made it self-evidently essential to keep daughters under the strict control of their fathers and wives under that of their husbands, and to shut widows away in nunneries such as Fontevraud. At the end of the twelfth century, every man who knew how the duchess of Aquitaine had behaved saw in her the exemplar of what both tempted and disturbed him in femininity.

Eleanor's fate, in fact, differed little from that of the

women of high birth whom chance, by depriving them of a brother, had made heiresses to a lordship. Hopes of the power which they transmitted excited greed. Would-be husbands quarrelled over them, competing to gain a foothold in their house and exploit their patrimony until the sons they would give them came of age. They were, consequently, relentlessly married and remarried as long as they were capable of giving birth. Eleanor's story is exceptional only in the two events, the divorce and the rebellion, events whose chief interest is to have provoked, because she was a queen and involved in high politics, the flurry of written commentaries from which historians can learn something about the condition of women at that time, which normally eludes their investigations. We know very little about Eleanor; there is no portrait and there are, as I have said, nine and only nine testimonies of any length, which are, in the last analysis, pretty thin; yet we know a lot more about her than about most women of her time.

Like all girls, Eleanor, at thirteen, had reached the age to be married, and her father chose the man she had never seen to whom she was given. The latter came to the paternal home to collect her. After the wedding, he took her straight back to his own home and, as was then the custom in pious families, the marriage was consummated, during the course of the journey, only after a devout delay of three days. Like all wives, Eleanor lived in a state of constant anxiety at her continued childlessness. Like many others, she was dispensed with because she was too long in producing a male child. Since she came from a distant province, and since her speech and some of her manners were surprising, she was regarded as an intruder by her husband's family, constantly spied on and slandered. At Antioch, it is certain that her Uncle Raymond exploited her, if not sexually, at least politically. He was the only man in the family; he therefore exercised over her the power of a father. It may well be that he persuaded her to demand the separation from Louis on grounds of consanguinity with the intention of then marrying her himself, in pursuit of his own interests. In the great noble houses, where hordes of people milled about and privacy was a rarity, there were always wives who succumbed to the approaches of their husband's seneschal. To all of them, in any case, the house poets, to please the husbands, dedicated their works, flattering the ladies with sycophantic praise, without, in actual fact, being their lovers. Women went from one pregnancy to another. This was what happened to Eleanor as soon as she was married to Henry Plantagenet. She had given Louis VII only two daughters; she provided Henry with three more daughters and five sons. Between her twenty-ninth and thirty-fourth years, impregnated every twelve months, she brought five children into the world. The rate then slackened. In 1165, she gave birth to the last of her children known to historians because they went to full term and, with one exception, survived beyond puberty. This was the tenth, in two decades. She was forty-one. Her reproductive capacity, like that of all the married women of her world, had been exploited to the full. Like them, after the menopause she assumed the role of matron, exploiting her power over her sons, tyrannizing her daughters-in-law, leaving her officials to administer her dower, planning the marriage of her granddaughters, who included Blanche of Castile, herself, in the next century, another impossible mother-in-law. Like all widows of her rank, she eventually withdrew to devote herself to a third husband, this one celestial, in the abbey on which her family had showered favours; she had done so herself during her lifetime, in order to purge her faults, for example after her divorce. The abbey was Fontevraud. William the Troubadour, her grandfather, had repeatedly mocked it, but he too, late in life, had bestowed gifts on it. Henry was already there, under the sod. She had escorted Richard's remains to it. There Eleanor lies, waiting for the Last Judgement.

What many people really thought of her in England can be seen from the way in which the chroniclers interpreted the tragic death of Henry II, in July 1189. How could God have let such a powerful sovereign die betrayed by all his legitimate sons, let him be carried naked to his tomb, stripped of everything by his servants, and allowed him to be buried in

the abbey of Fontevraud which he had not chosen for his
tomb? Admittedly, he too had enriched it with donations,
but because he longed with all his heart for Eleanor to take
the veil there and finally cease to be a thorn in his side. In the
book he wrote 'on the instruction of princes', Gerald of
Wales said that God might have been punishing the murderer
of Thomas Becket and the descendant of the fairy Melusine,
daughter of Satan. He was certainly punishing Henry for the
sins of his wife, chief among them bigamy. No one doubted
that Eleanor was a bigamist, and doubly incestuous. Cousin
of Henry Plantagenet in the same degree as the Capetian
king, both of her two marriages were culpable. Henry had
been a willing partner. God was exacting his revenge. But he
was punishing him primarily for incest 'of the second type',
the terrible sin he had committed under the baneful charms
of Eleanor, instrument of the devil.

How some, and probably many, people viewed the duchess
of Aquitaine in the courts of northern France can be seen
from the long and racy romance that enjoyed such a huge
success in the last decades of the twelfth century, the *Roman
de Renart*. Who, listening to its account of the misfortunes
of Isengrin, was not reminded of the marital problems that
had beset Louis VII at Antioch, which people still laughed
about thirty years later, deriding the husband who was 'so
jealous that he thought he was always being cuckolded',
whose mistake had been to wash his dirty linen in public, to
have shamelessly 'execrated his wife', when 'that sort of
thing was best kept quiet'? Who, throughout this scintillating, mocking story, could not think of Eleanor herself as they
heard about the three ladies whose 'grapes' had been joyfully
'trodden' by that 'great fornicator', Reynard? First, Herme-
line who, as soon as she thought she was rid of her husband,
went off, 'hugging and kissing' the young man she had lined
up as her new husband and new lord, whom she had chosen
because she already knew that he 'did it very well'? And
who, hearing about the queen, the wife of the lion, the proud
Lady Fière, whom Reynard enjoyed one night when, furious
with her husband, she was sleeping apart, did not remember
the good fortune of Geoffrey Plantagenet when he visited the

French court? Was not Eleanor, too, scorning the advice of the wise ('Let God guard you from dishonour'), inclined to give her ring to young men in the hope that they would soon come 'for the love' promised by this pledge, 'to talk to her privately and discreetly'? And did not the poet, exploiting the persistence of the scandal, make sure that his listeners recognized Queen Eleanor in the features of Hersent the adulteress, Hersent the temptress, the wily one, reproaching the gallants from the bed on which she had just given birth for being too fearful of her husband's anger, for not visiting her as often as she wanted in her room, and, obligingly, readily indulging in all the pleasures of the game? For Hersent, this game was almost her reason for living, and she left Isengrin, her husband, when he revealed that he was no longer a man: 'since he can't do it, what use is he to me?'; Hersent was a 'whore', who, 'having one husband took another' – in other words she was a bigamist.

The thoughts of anyone who heard Eleanor mentioned at this period turned to sex, which was the principal theme of *Renart* in the most scintillating of its social critique. Eleanor-Hermeline, Eleanor-Fière, Eleanor-Hersent, this woman was the incarnation of lust and 'lechery'. She thought of nothing else, and, basically, men connived, since for them woman was a plaything, all the more attractive if she was consumed by desire. But what was important was that she respected the rules of the game behind which sex was concealed; that things happened discreetly, without fuss and without violence. And without complaints: the man who was criticized was Louis VII, who, incapable of himself slaking the passions of his partner, had the bad taste to be jealous. Reynard, on the other hand, was forgiven because he loved, and for his expertise in love – courtly love, of course. When a lady responded to their advances, and accepted their 'love', men were justified in pursuing her and in taking her. Eleanor was an excellent excuse. Her supposed behaviour justified every excess and one might make free with her in spite of her marriage. This is probably why Andrew the Chaplain put her in his *Treatise on Love*, another burlesque, seated in the middle of a court of love, in the role of imaginary and risible legislator for the rules of courtesy. It is unfortunate that such jokes, like the bombastic eulogies of the troubadours, have been, and are still today, taken seriously. Should one celebrate Eleanor's virtues? Or should one mock or wax indignant at her faults? For my part, I am inclined, rather, to pity her.

2

Mary Magdalen

In the middle of the twelfth century, a little book was written for the use of pilgrims to St James of Compostella. It was not unlike the tourist brochures distributed by travel agencies today; for the four routes that traversed the kingdom of France and merged to cross the Pyrenees, it noted which sanctuaries were worth a visit, even a detour, because they sheltered other saints as powerful, or almost, as the apostle James; of this, the miracles which occurred near their tomb were proof. Among these healers and protectors were two women, St Faith and St Mary Magdalen; the former lay at Conques, the latter at Vézelay.

Vézelay was then a key point in the network of devout pilgrimages. One of the four 'routes of St James' started from it, and St Bernard chose to preach the second crusade in this busy spot at about the same time that the *Pilgrim's Guide* was produced. The *Guide* briefly praised the town's attractions. These included, it said, 'an imposing and very beautiful basilica'; this was the church, then nearly complete, which we still marvel at today. It was the scene of splendid festivities on 22 July, because it contained 'the very holy body of the blessed Mary Magdalen', of 'that glorious Mary who ... washed with her tears the feet of the Lord ... for which her many sins were forgiven her because she so loved him who loved all men, Jesus, her redeemer'. Among other good deeds, the saint restored sight to the blind, speech to the dumb, movement to the paralysed and tranquillity to those possessed by demons, which were the miracles that Christ himself had performed. Last, but not least, 'out of love of her, the Lord forgave sinners their sins'. It was all there: cures, sin, love, tears and redemption, enough to explain the dazzling success of the pilgrimage, then one of the most popular in the West, the crowds of people, the enrichment of the monastic community and the wonderful church; enough also to explain the insistent presence in the collective imagination of a female figure, that of the lover of God, the woman pardoned, famous everywhere thanks to vigorous publicity and the tales of pilgrims. In the twelfth century, Mary Magdalen was alive and present as much as Eleanor of Aquitaine. And the hopes and fears of men were projected onto her imagined body, just as they were onto the body of Eleanor.

Many women appear in the Gospel stories. Mentioned eighteen times, Mary Magdalen is the most visible of all, the one whose attitudes and feelings are described most fully, much less unobtrusive and abstract, much more liberated from the legendary, than the other Mary, the Mother of God. 'Mary, surnamed Magdalen', from whom, says Luke, 'seven devils had been cast out', had served Jesus in Galilee. With a few companions who, like her, had been cured by him of an evil spirit or illness, she had followed Jesus to Jerusalem and accompanied him even to Golgotha. From a distance, these devoted followers had watched the Crucifixion. Then, when the body of Christ Crucified had been taken down and placed in the tomb, they wanted to anoint it with spices. Tending the bodies of the dead was then women's work, which was still the case in the twelfth century. They had to wait, however, for the end of the sabbath to buy the perfumes. On Easter morning, at sunrise, they returned to the sepulchre to find it open and the stone rolled aside. Frightened, they ran off and told the Apostles. Peter and John came running, Mary Magdalen with them. They established that the body was no longer there and left. Mary alone remained, weeping, at the threshold of the tomb. 'Why weepest thou?' asked two angels. 'Because they have taken away my Lord, and I know not where they have laid him.' As she spoke, she turned and saw a man she took for the gardener. When he called her by name, Mary, she recognized him as Jesus. She wanted to detain him, but he prevented her and told her to announce the Resurrection to his disciples. Mary Magdalen was the first witness of the Resurrection, hence the apostle of the Apostles.

The Gospels mention two other women who can be confused with Mary Magdalen. One, anonymous, was 'a woman in the city, which was a sinner', that is, a harlot. Luke presents her in the house of a Pharisee in Galilee, where Jesus was taking a meal. She 'stood at his feet behind him weeping, and began to wash his feet with tears, and did wipe them with the hairs of her head, and kissed his feet, and anointed them with the ointment.' 'This man, if he were a prophet,' said the Pharisee, 'would have known who and what manner of woman this is.' Jesus answered: 'Her sins are forgiven . . . for she loved much.' This is the passage that the author of the *Guide* summarized. But he located the scene elsewhere, no longer in Galilee but in Judaea, at Bethany, just before the Passion, in the house of Simon the Leper. The confusion is understandable, since Mark and Matthew situate a very similar episode in this house: Jesus was at table; a woman approached him with 'an alabaster box of ointment of spikenard very precious; and she brake the box and poured it on his head'. To Judas Iscariot, who was enraged, saying it would have been better to give the money to the poor, Jesus replied: 'Let her alone . . . she is come aforehand to anoint my body to the burying.' John, who also describes this event, specifies that the woman bringing the ointment was called Mary. She was the sister of Martha and Lazarus, close friends of Jesus, at whose feet Luke describes her sitting, drinking in his words, whilst Martha busied herself in the kitchen and grumbled.

So we have three different women. All three, however, poured, or were preparing to pour, a perfume over the body of the living Jesus (or the dead Jesus, but it was the same, as he himself observed). All three are shown prostrate before the master, kneeling, in a posture of contemplation and of loving adoration. In the sixth century, therefore, Pope Gregory the Great felt justified in claiming in his Homilies, especially the Thirty-third, that 'the woman described by Luke as the sinner, called Mary by John, is the same woman of whom Mark says that she was liberated from seven devils.' Throughout the Middle Ages, there were very few people who hesitated to accept this claim.

At least, this was the case in Latin Christendom. The Greek Church continued to distinguish Mary Magdalen from the other two. It celebrated her feast on 22 July and venerated her tomb at Ephesus. From the eastern Mediterranean, by way of southern Italy, the cult of the saint spread in the West, initially in England. The first traces of it appear in this country – closely linked to Rome since its recent conversion and, as a result, to the Byzantine sources – in the eighth century. Its Benedictine monasteries were then in the vanguard of the spiritual quest, and missionaries from these abbeys carried the seeds of the devotion to Mary Magdalen to the Continent. In return, it was probably in the great Frankish monasteries, notably Saint-Benoît-sur-Loire, then a prolific workshop of liturgical innovation, that, starting from the readings of the nocturnal office on Easter Sunday, a piece of theatre took shape; Archbishop Dunstan of Canterbury described a performance of it at the end of the tenth century. In this early essay in sacred drama, Mary Magdalen became physically present within the church. On Good Friday, a cross wrapped in a veil, representing the dead Christ, was placed on the altar in a reliquary, simulacrum of the Holy Sepulchre. It was removed during the night of Saturday, leaving only the veil, that is, the shroud. At the beginning of the Easter mass, a monk, dressed like the angel in a white alb, took up a position at the right of the tomb; three other monks, miming the actions of the holy women, stepped forward; between them and the first monk, a few sentences were exchanged, those of St Mark's Gospel: 'Who do you seek? – Jesus of Nazareth – He is risen; he is not here.' These are the remote origins of our theatre. For, and this is the crucial point, this dialogue was gradually extended, whilst the Easter liturgies were enriched and the person of Mary Magdalen began to stand out from the group of holy women. In a manuscript from Tours, which is contemporary with the *Pilgrim's Guide*, she now occupies centre stage. She approaches the open tomb alone, she proclaims her grief, she falls into a swoon at the conclusion of a long and loving lament, and her companions arrive to lift her up. 'Dear sister, there is too much affliction in your soul.' By the mid-twelfth century, it is probable that the spectacle had already emerged from the cloister and become public. For a long time, however, it had remained confined to the monastic milieu where, let us not forget, it was a man who took the role of Mary, the friend of the Lord.

It was also a male monastery that produced the oldest of the texts composed, by a man, to be read on 22 July, the day when the saint was celebrated, before men. This 'sermon to venerate Mary Magdalen' is traditionally attributed to Eudes, abbot of Cluny at the beginning of the tenth century. In fact, neither its author nor its date is known, and the most convincing hypothesis is that it was composed a century later, in Burgundy. It is a commentary on the Gospel text, organized according to the deductive techniques employed by the scholars in the abbey of Saint-Germain of Auxerre at the end of the Carolingian period. It was intended to bring out the meaning of the words, their many meanings, in order to draw a moral lesson from Scripture. Through it, we get an insight into the image formed by one monk, around the year 1000, of a female figure whom he was describing to other monks for their spiritual enlightenment.

It was certainly a woman he described. It was as a woman – the word *mulier* keeps recurring – that Mary Magdalen was celebrated. But what sort of woman? Was it the sinner? Not at all; the unknown author of the sermon saw her as a woman who had lived, but who had eventually detached herself from earthly things to draw closer to those of heaven. This woman was rich and generous (*largissime*), because she was of high birth (*clarissime*) and disposed freely of her own property. The features ascribed to her by this cleric, who also came from the very highest aristocracy, were those of the women amongst whom he had spent his childhood, those of widowed princesses such as Adelaide, wife and mother of emperors, whose epitaph was then being composed by Abbot Odilo of Cluny, or those of the dowagers who, at that period, did everything in their power to support the monastic institution, the only women with whom the monks could associate without shame. Deprived by age of the disturbing charms of femininity, they had once shared the bed of a man, known pleasure, and hence sinned. Now retired, they wept for their sins. The author of the sermon emphasized these female tears (though the link between tears, sin and remission would be most clearly brought out when he spoke of Lazarus, here representing the Resurrection). For him, Mary Magdalen was guilty, admittedly, but as we all are. To sin is the lot of the human race. Without the quotation from the Gospel, who would have thought of a prostitute? The author's discretion suggests that the obsession with sexual stain and uneasiness in the face of women to some extent spared these men, who had been offered as children to a monastery, who had never left it, and who had consequently remained virgins.

Accordingly, the female nature is not defined in this text by the inclination to lust, but by two other features. The first was weakness and timidity. This made it possible to present Mary Magdalen as an example to men. Though a woman, had she not mastered her weakness and her fear? She alone had remained before the open tomb. The second and crucial feature was love, 'the fervent ardour of love', and this outpouring of femininity is here presented as a prime virtue. It underpinned the constancy and perseverance she demonstrated. Mary Magdalen wept, but it was not from remorse. She wept from unsatisfied desire, desire for this man 'who, living, she loved with too great a love'. Throwing herself at the feet of Jesus was the act of a lover, not of a penitent. Burning with love for her master, Mary went to the sepulchre. Finding it empty, she persevered. Because she did not cease to search, to wait in the shadows, overcoming her fear and her doubts, she deserved to see. Yes, we men, we should become women, and cultivate in us what there is of the feminine in order to love fully, as is right.

There follows, in this monastic text, a sort of rehabilitation of femininity, in homage, perhaps, to those noble widows to whom the monks were constantly repeating that they were capable, more so than their dead husband, of touching God. For having loved, waited and hoped, a woman had deserved, despite her weaknesses (here, masculine condescension, the invincible pride of being a man, slips out), to announce the miracle to the Apostles. This was a signal honour which, said the sermon, vividly demonstrated 'the very merciful benevolence of the Lord regarding womankind'. Death had entered this world through one woman, Eve. Another woman, Mary, mother of God, had opened the gates of Paradise. Here, midway between these two stood one who was accessible and imitable, a sinner like all women, Mary Magdalen. Rich, benevolent and generous, God had wanted his victory over death to be announced by her. Because of her, by the divine will, 'the opprobrium which weighed on the female sex had been lifted'.

At this period, scholarly thinking proceeded by leaps, from word to word or from image to image. Other images, therefore, that of the monastic community, and that of the ecclesial institution as a whole, were inevitably suggested by the image of this woman, and it was by insisting on these that the homily developed its lesson. It emphasized above all an act more eloquent than any word: the sinner, prostrated in the house of the Pharisee, said nothing; she knelt. This posture of humiliation, of self-surrender, also of love, played a central role in the rites of passage then marking the conversion or the transformation of a life. In the rite of marriage, the affianced woman knelt before her husband, before the man she would in future call her lord. In the rite of vassalic engagement, the vassal knelt before him who received him as his man. It appears, lastly, in the rite of monastic profession as it is described in the Cluniac custumals. This act imposed obedience and it imposed service. Like the new wife, like the new vassal, and like the monk who had completed his noviciate, Mary Magdalen changed

her life and was veritably reborn. Kneeling, she expressed
her desire to enter into service 'not only in spirit but in body',
and she was effectively 'accepted', received and incorporated
into the house of a master, into his *familia*, into his team of
servants and protegées, those from whom he expected obedience and whom he sustained with his favours. By this act,
the image of Mary Magdalen invited the men who listened
to the sermon to surrender themselves to the will of the Lord
in order to serve him, and splendidly, as she had done.

Here, the text appears to be directed against the critics
who proliferated with the approach of the millennium and
who were hounded as heretics. Against the most disturbing
of them, this female figure affirmed the truth of the Incarnation and of Redemption. Against all of them, she further
affirmed that it was not wrong for a monastery to be rich,
since this is what Mary Magdalen had been. The word
Magdala meant tower or castle, and evoked dominating
structures, painstakingly constructed of finely dressed
masonry, such as the bell-towers which it was at this period
being decided to build at Saint-Benoît-sur-Loire and Saint-
Germain-des-Prés. With her gifts, Mary Magdalen had supported men who owned nothing: Jesus and his disciples. She
had been prodigal and spent without counting the cost,
squandering the precious perfume before an appalled Judas.
The heretics were Judases when they condemned the wealth
of the Church. To pour perfume was to build, decorate and
set out to cover Christendom in a white mantle of new
churches. The monks of that period felt they were obliged,
like Martha and Mary in the house of their brother Lazarus,
to receive 'the nobles and the powerful in the dignity of
secular pomp'. Mary Magdalen justified them.

Lastly, just as the scent of the perfume had spread from
the dining-table to pervade Simon's entire house, so, from
the monastery, the requirements of submission, of service
and of love ought to spread to the whole Church. If the
monks followed the example of Mary, the friend of Jesus of
Nazareth, they would in their turn set an example to the
clergy and to the members of the secular Church. For the
latter was, indeed, guilty; it, too, ought to kneel, to be

converted and solemnly to renounce the old, unclean life. Composed in veneration of Mary Magdalen, the sermon called for the general reform of the ecclesiastical institution. At the beginning of the eleventh century, this reform was under way, and, under the impulse of the papacy, it was gathering pace. Mary Magdalen inevitably became one of its emblematic figures. When the reformers founded two communities of canons, models for the clergy of regular and pure life, one in Lorraine, at Verdun, in 1023, the other in Burgundy, at Besançon, in 1048, they dedicated both to Mary Magdalen. It was at this moment that a rumour began to circulate to the effect that her body lay not far away, at Vézelay.

When he founded the abbey at Vézelay, around 860, Gerard of Roussillon dedicated it only to Christ, the Virgin and St Peter. There is nothing to suggest that the monks of Vézelay had previously claimed to preserve even the tiniest fragment of the remains of Mary Magdalen. Suddenly, a text composed between 1037 and 1043 affirmed against detractors that these remains were there, that the many apparitions and marvels occurring on the tomb were proof and, lastly, that pilgrims were already flooding in from the whole of Gaul in search of miracles. There can be no doubt that it was in the second quarter of the eleventh century that the relics were 'invented', as it was then put – that is to say, discovered.

It was universally believed, at this period, that the saints remained present on earth, and powerful, in what remained of their body. These remains were generally regarded as the most effective agents of the very necessary contact between the living and the celestial court where the Almighty sat in judgement. Holy bodies were turning up all over Europe at this time. The chronicler Raoul Glaber, a very well-informed man then writing in Burgundy, roundly denounced the fabricators of false relics. He nevertheless celebrated these desirable discoveries as one of the most convincing demonstrations of the generosity of God, finally reconciled with his people after the calamities of the millennium of his Passion. However, also at this period – and it is this that was new –

the attention of ruling Church circles began to turn firmly
towards the New Testament texts. They probably still
encouraged the veneration of the local saints, the martyrs of
Rome, the first missionaries and those protectors who, near
sacred springs, had long since been substituted for the
tutelary divinities of pre-Christian times. But they now
oriented the devotion of the faithful towards the persons
who appeared in the Gospel stories and the Acts of the
Apostles. Latin Christendom, however, possessed practically
nothing of the bodies of these particular saints. It was this
dearth, together with the new concern to be linked, if I may
use the expression, bodily, with the apostolic age through
the intermediary of those who had seen, heard and followed
the living Jesus, that made the pilgrimages to Rome and to
Compostella so popular; with St Peter, St James was the only
one of the Twelve Apostles to have been buried in Western
Europe. This scarcity also encouraged scholars to try to
attach more closely to the person of Christ various saints
whose remains had lain for centuries in the reliquaries of
Gaul, to prove at all costs, for example, that Martial of
Limoges, protector of Aquitaine, had been, if not an apostle,
at least one of the first disciples, or that Denis of Montmartre,
confused with Denis the Areopagite, had received instruction
directly from St Paul. One can then understand why princes
celebrated as a magnificent gift from heaven the discovery of
the head of St John the Baptist at Saint-Jean-d'Angély. It also
explains the discovery, at this same period, of the relics of
Mary Magdalen at Vézelay and, simultaneously, the relics of
her brother Lazarus at Autun.

In the case of Vézelay and Mary Magdalen, the reform
movement played a decisive role. In 1037, a new abbot,
Geoffrey, was elected. Inspired by the customs of Cluny, one
of his first concerns was to restore order to the old monastery, where morals had deteriorated. For the restoration to
be solidly based, the abbey had to be prosperous, therefore
people must admire it and feel for it that gratitude that
ensured a steady flow of alms. It needed, therefore, to possess
some remarkable and effective relics. As a good adminis-
trator, Geoffrey ordered the compilation of a collection of

miracles – this is the text I have been discussing – in order to launch the pilgrimage. It was he who 'invented' the relics. But why, when there is nothing at Cluny, which he took as his model and which supported his action, to suggest that Mary Magdalen had till then been the object of a special veneration, did Geoffrey recognize in one of the sarcophagi with a barely legible epitaph found in his abbey that of this saint rather than that of some other famous miracle-worker? It was, perhaps, because the fame of this servant of the Lord was beginning to grow in the West, but it was primarily because she had become, in the region, the patron of general reform. And Geoffrey was a keen reformer; indeed, this was why he had been appointed. He was one of the promoters of the truce of God in Burgundy. In 1049, the year when the churches of the Madeleine at Verdun and at Besançon were consecrated by Pope Leo IX, Geoffrey was at Reims, at the pope's side, in a council whose purpose, in deposing fornicating prelates and condemning incestuous and bigamous princes, was to suppress sin, and in particular sexual sins, at the summit of the social edifice. The following year, Geoffrey was at Rome for a similar gathering and, in the bull he obtained in favour of his monastery, on 27 April, the usual formula was modified in such a way as to specify that Vézelay was still dedicated to Christ, the Virgin and SS Peter and Paul, but also to St Mary Magdalen. Eight years later, a further bull solemnly confirmed that Mary Magdalen did indeed 'repose' at Vézelay. In 1108, lastly, in the privilege granted to this monastery by Pope Pascal II, the old patrons were forgotten, and only Mary Magdalen appeared. The pilgrimage was now a huge success. It had triggered off, throughout Latin Christendom, what historians have called an 'explosion' in the cult of the saint.

For this cult to be celebrated worthily, there had to be a body of 'legends' in the original meaning of the word, that is of texts intended to be read during the offices. Three stories were added to the sermon I discussed above. They were complementary to the Gospel story, responding to two questions: what had happened to Mary Magdalen between the time when the risen Christ appeared to her and the time

of her own death? And how had it come about (and many
people, the miracle collection as admitted, had wondered
about this) that the body of this woman, born in Judaea, had
been transported to Gaul from so distant a region? To
answer the first question, which was already asked by
pilgrims to Ephesus, a story, the life that is called eremitic,
had been developed in the East. It was based on the biography of a repentant prostitute, another Mary, the Egyptian,
one of those sunburned, blackened, hairy women whom the
hermits of ancient Thebes imagined to be, like them, purging
their faults in the desert. This story, as it was read in the
communities of anchorites in southern Italy, and as, from
there, it reached English monasteries by the eighth century,
goes as follows:

> After the Ascension of the Saviour, transformed by a burning
> love for the Lord and by the sorrow she felt after his death,
> [Mary Magdalen] wished never again to see with her own
> eyes a man or a human being; [she] withdrew for some thirty
> years into the desert, unknown to anyone, never eating human
> food or drinking. At every canonical hour, the angels of the
> Lord came down from the sky and raised her up with them
> into the air so that she could pray in their company.

One day, a priest saw some angels fluttering above a closed
cave. He approached and called out. Without showing
herself, Mary Magdalen made herself known and explained
the miracle to him. She asked him to bring her some clothes
because 'she could not appear naked among men'. He
returned and took her to the church where he celebrated
mass. There she died, after having communicated with the
body and the blood of Jesus Christ. 'Through her holy
merits, great marvels soon occurred near to her tomb.'

At the time when Geoffrey was battling to get it accepted
that this tomb was to be found in his abbey, another life of
Mary Magdalen was circulating, the one that historians call
apostolic. It claimed that, after Pentecost, Mary had set sail
in the company of Maximin, one of the seventy-two disciples.
Disembarking at Marseilles, the two of them set out to

evangelize the region round Aix by their preaching. When Mary Magdalen died, Maximin gave her a beautiful funeral and placed her body in a sarcophagus of marble, on one side of which was carved the scene of the meal in the house of Simon. It was possible to reconcile this second legend with the first by placing the desert described in the latter in the mountains of Provence, in the Sainte-Baume. This second text, nevertheless, worried the Burgundian monks. It located the tomb close to Aix, where, in fact, the growth of the cult of Mary Magdalen is attested before the beginning of the twelfth century and where a rival pilgrimage may already have been developing. To silence those who refused to see them as the true guardians of the relics, they fabricated a story – this is the third legend – recounting that a monk, on the orders of Gerard of Roussillon and the first abbot, had gone and stolen them away three centuries earlier when Provence was being ravaged by the Saracens.

These complementary legends provided the material with which to give more solid support to the initiatives of the reformers. The example of Mary Magdalen in the desert encouraged the secular Church in particular, which was next to be purified, to move further away from the carnal world, to forget it, to forget its body, as she had done, in order to join the angelic choir in a posture of loving contemplation, so that it could better fulfil its mission to teach. Indeed, a detail in the second story emphasized the need to purify oneself: no king or prince could enter the basilica built by Maximin over her tomb unless he had first put aside his military accoutrements and his warlike intentions. And access was strictly prohibited to women – an exclusion that alone, let us note, rules out any suggestion that the rise of the cult of Mary Magdalen had some connection with an alleged upgrading of the position of women. No arms, that is to say bloodshed, and no women, that is to say sexual excess: these were the two major stains from which Pope Leo IX, Geoffrey of Vézelay and his friends, preaching the peace of God and prohibiting incest and bigamy, were then attempting to liberate the great of this world, both ecclesiastical and lay. Nevertheless, like the tenth/eleventh-century

sermon, these legends did not emphasize sin or redemption.
They did not say that Mary Magdalen had withdrawn into
solitude there to weep for her faults and mortify herself. It
was passionate attachment and grief that had motivated her
in the painful memory of the lost love. They, too, put the
emphasis on love, ardent and ecstatic love.

Some decades later, at the beginning of the twelfth century,
in the sermon that another Geoffrey, abbot of the great
monastery of the Trinity in Vendôme, composed for the
benefit of the men under his authority, the features emphasized are quite different. The following are what seem to me
the main features of his homily:

1 It is almost wholly based on the scene described in St
Luke's Gospel of the meal in the house of the Pharisee.
2 Taking sides in a very topical and fierce debate, Geoffrey
condemns the Pharisee who wanted to chastise the sinner: 'a
man without mercy,' he says, 'who despised women, who
regarded them as excluded from salvation and who would
not allow himself to be touched by them'.
3 Mary Magdalen, says Geoffrey of Vendôme, was first 'a
famous sinner, then a glorious preacher'. Closely following
the text of the life called apostolic, he shows her 'assiduously
preaching Our Lord Jesus Christ, true God, and attesting to
the truth of his resurrection'. He is specific, however, that
the saint bore witness 'more by tears than by words'.
4 Last but not least, the woman that Geoffrey presents as
an example was above all the one who was beset by seven
devils, that is by all the vices. A sinner (the word appears
fourteen times in this short text), *peccatrix*, but also *accusa-
trix*, conscious of her faults and confessing them, crouched
at the feet of the master. She was pardoned, certainly, but by
reason of the excess, not, here, of her love, on which Geoffrey
puts little emphasis, but of her fear and her hope. Furthermore, abandoned, submissive, as women should always be,
Mary Magdalen was nevertheless only fully redeemed after
having done penance. Interpreting in his own way the
eremitical life, Geoffrey asserted that, after the Ascension,

she had attacked her own body, punishing it with fasts, vigils and continuous prayer. As a result of this voluntary violence, Mary Magdalen, 'victim' and 'stubborn victim', was established on the threshold of salvation, 'gatekeeper of heaven'. *Hostia, ostiaria*, the two Latin words echo each other; it was, as I have said, by the play of assonances that the deductions of the learned proceeded at this period.

We should note, however, that in two other works by Geoffrey of Vendôme – a sermon and a letter addressed to the bishop of Le Mans, Hildebert of Lavardin – the same allegory, that of the gatekeeper, appears, and it is again the female sex that performs this role. But the gate opened here is that of sin and of the fall. Woman, all women, the maidservant of the high priest before whom St Peter denied Christ, Eve in Paradise urging Adam to disobey, were the instruments of the devil. Through them, damnation had entered this world. Steeped in sin, as they all were, Mary Magdalen, before she could become the hope of all sinners and procure a place at the gate of heaven and no longer of hell, had been obliged wholly to destroy and consume with mortifications the female part of her being. It is at this particular point that the emphasis has shifted.

How are we to explain that, for the image of a rich and powerful woman, so carried away by her passion she subjected herself to the man she loved, was prostrated by grief when she thought he was dead, and then went out and proclaimed in the highways and byways that he had triumphed over death, there was substituted the image of one who was a carrier of evil, ravaged by remorse, destroying her body with physical abuse? For enlightenment, we need to turn to that major development in Latin Christendom between 1075 and 1125, the success of ecclesiastical reform. The purification, after monasticism, of the secular Church, and the imposition on it of monastic morality, had effectively resulted in dividing men – and here I mean men – into two categories: on the one hand, those for whom resort to women was strictly forbidden; on the other, those who ought to possess one, but only one, legitimate woman, and, sullied by that very fact, were located in the hierarchy of merits below the asexual and, consequently, subject to their power. This segregation marked the culture of Western Europe in a way that has never been wholly eradicated, entrenching deep in people's consciousness for centuries the idea that the source of sin was in the first place sex. As a result, in 1100, reform came up against a major obstacle and stumbling-block: women.

This was firstly because the men who, under papal leadership, pursued the policy of purification, the bishops, the good bishops who had been appointed after the impenitent depraved had been driven out, were often, like Hildebert of Lavardin, friend of Geoffrey of Vendôme, reformed former fornicators. They had experienced the 'voluptuous pleasures' that had to be stamped out. They had been obliged, not without difficulty, to reform themselves. They were struggling finally to rid themselves of their own guilt, and perhaps the memory of the *meretriculae tabernae*, of the 'little tavern whores' of their youth, still occasionally haunted them. They had an instinctive tendency to regard women as prostitutes, real or virtual. This explains the obsessive metaphors which flowed from the pens of the great scholars of the Val de Loire when they wrote about women: a womb, voracious, a chimera, a monster. The fault lay in what the writers were conscious of resisting in their own body that was female, that is, animal.

Furthermore, these prelates, in the course of their pastoral duties, were constantly confronted with the concrete problems posed by women. Prostitution flourished in the rapidly expanding towns, thronging with uprooted immigrants. Above all, there were those women without men that the reform movement itself had thrown out on the street, the wives abandoned by husbands because they were priests, or if laymen, because they were bigamists or had contracted an incestuous union. These women were to be pitied, but they were also dangerous, threatening to corrupt men and lead them astray. What should be their place in the perfect society that was the aim of the reformers? Many of them, including, as his judgement on the Pharisee shows, Geoffrey of Vendôme, believed that it was necessary to be concerned for their souls, to accept them as they were accepted in heretical circles, and so to develop for their benefit an appropriate pastoral mission; this might be risky, but it was inescapable. But how far could one go? What about Robert of Arbrissel? He welcomed women into his company, trailing them in his wake as Jesus had done, and, in the mixed monastery of Fontevraud, put them in positions over the monks, enjoining the latter to demean themselves to serve them, and to accept this humiliation in order to win the love of Christ, their husband, in the same way that the knight who courteously served the lady hoped to win the love of the husband, his lord. This was surely going too far. And was the same not true of Abelard when he claimed that the prayers of the women at the Paraclete were worth as much as those of the men? Abelard was reviled by Bernard of Clairvaux, who accused him of too much 'talking to women'. The volume of the imprecations hurled against those men of the Church who got too close to women, and who could not, it was assumed, escape sin, attest to the scale of the malaise, the strength of the reservations and the irrepressible fear of sexual stain. How many prelates continued to think that it was proper to keep women at arm's length from the sacred, and forbid them access to certain sanctuaries? To that of Menat, in Auvergne, for example, which Robert of Arbrissel eventually managed to throw open to them, ceaselessly asserting that, communicating in the body of Christ like men, women had the right to enter like them into his house? Or even to the tomb of Mary Magdalen in Provence?

The rulers of the Church, in any case, were as one in believing that it was necessary to prevent women from doing damage, hence to confine them, by marrying them off. The perfect woman – and here the attitude of Mary Magdalen was exemplary – was, in effect, one who depended totally on her lord, who cherished but above all feared him, and who also served him; in fact, the woman who wept but held her tongue, who obeyed, prostrated before her man. Consequently, with the onset of puberty, the girl should become a wife, either the wife of a master who would keep her on a tight rein, or else of Christ, enclosed in a convent. If not, the odds were she would become a whore. Like men, women were divided into two groups, and again on a sexual criterion: *uxores-meretrices*; matrons or prostitutes. This is why the good bishops such as Hildebert of Lavardin and Marbode of Rennes chose, at this period, to rewrite the lives of repentant prostitutes who were so fully and so perfectly mortified in the powers of their baneful seduction that they could become saints, celebrated as such for having voluntarily ravaged themselves, like Mary the Egyptian, or like Thaïs. And, in order to dissuade men from the capital sin, these prelates presented woman in the guise that was for them most terrifying, as temptress, decked out in all her finery, accosting men and luring them into what was most despicable in the union of bodies. They wanted in this way to prove that the soul, however contaminated by lust, could be washed spotlessly clean by bodily penance. This is why there appeared, at this period, new Thaïs, the recluses, who established themselves not in the desert, but in town centres, shut away in a cell, from which they bore witness, teaching and preaching. But they preached without words, by the ruin of their bodies alone. This is why the Mary Magdalen of Geoffrey of Vendôme so closely resembles Mary the Egyptian; and it is why sinners beseeched her, mingling their tears with hers, and why so many people climbed the hill of Vézelay, knowing, as they were told by the *Pilgrims' Guide*, that the Lord would forgive them their sins for her sake. As a mediator, she was listened to because she was a stubborn penitent.

It was, in fact, at the beginning of the twelfth century that the instrument the Church hoped to use to deepen moral reform and constrain all of the faithful to obey its precepts took shape, that is the sacrament of penance. The rite demanded not only contrition and confession, but also, basing itself on the practices of public justice, and extending to society as a whole procedures of atonement in use in monastic communities for centuries, redemption. It required one to pay, to 'satisfy' the judge by submitting to a punishment. And so the idea gained ground of a tariff, of a gradation of redeeming punishments, hence of a place, a time of waiting, purgatories, and of an accounting managed by the administrators of the sacred, the priests. Meanwhile, the act of Jesus – pardoning for one reason alone: love – was relegated to the background and gradually eclipsed. In this way, the bodily appearance of the woman who loved Jesus more passionately than anyone else came primarily to represent, in the collective imagination, sin and its redemption. During the twelfth and thirteenth centuries, these features became fixed, as the renown of the relics of Vézelay reached its apogee then gradually declined, as popular preaching flourished and the figure of Mary Magdalen became prominent in the piety of the new religious movements, Franciscan and Dominican, and as the success of the pilgrimage to Provence was confirmed, slowly at first, then rapidly after a new discovery, this time at Saint-Maximin, of the saint's remains. For many, Mary Magdalen no doubt remained the 'loving beauty'. The vocabulary of courtly love entered the various saints' Lives in the romance language which were more widely known thanks to the preachers: Magdalen, 'sweet lover', found, they said, in Christ, the 'true lover', whom 'she loved very ardently', 'courtesy, amiability and great sweetness'. And when St Louis, returning from Syria, disembarked in Provence in 1254, the place he visited in the Sainte-Baume, climbing right up to that 'vault of high rock, where Mary Magdalen, it was said, had spent seventeen years as a hermit', was perhaps for him one of mystical ecstasies rather than of mortifications. Nevertheless, since the time of Geoffrey of Vendôme and of Hildebert, sin, the sins of the flesh, expiated by physical self-destruction, occupied centre stage. The fact that, for the Gospel reading on 22 July, the episode of the Easter morning described by John was gradually replaced during the course of the thirteenth century by that of the meal in the house of the Pharisee described by Luke, and that the figure of the prostitute weeping for her faults supplanted that of the tearful lover, is striking proof.

The faithful, those who looked towards Vézelay and those who looked towards Saint-Maximin, saw primarily a Mary

Magdalen in tears. They saw a torrent of tears, indeed a flood of them: Mary Magdalen and Maximin 'burst into tears so copiously that by their tears not only was the floor of the chapel watered, but it was so thoroughly drenched that in some places water lay on the tiles' and, on her deathbed, Mary, 'dissolving into tears, received her creator in such a fashion that her eyes seemed to be two conduits of a fountain providing running water'. Jacques de Vitry, preaching on the theme of Mary Magdalen, was in no doubt; these were tears of contrition and their source was 'the sadness of sins'. Mary Magdalen was in future primarily the repentant prostitute. This is how she appeared in the models constructed by the masters of the Parisian schools for the use of the preachers, and in the writings which proliferated during the thirteenth century and reveal the intentions of the ecclesiastical apparatus with regard to the figure of the blessed woman that it wished to disseminate among the people.

For this reason, the sermons they composed on this theme were never aimed principally at women. From the end of the twelfth century, more and more women chose to imitate the acts of Mary Magdalen; they lived apart from the world, penitents, weeping and claiming that they, too, ate only the bread of the angels. It is striking how the preachers who collected their sayings and narrated their lives in the hope that, by extolling their merits, they would defuse the impact of the total renunciations made by married women in Cathar regions, judged it prudent not to evoke, in this connection the figure of Mary Magdalen. She could not be a model of female sanctity. What was then repeated to women was that they would be more or less generously rewarded for their good works according to whether they were ranked among the virgins, among the widows or among the wives. Not a virgin, not a wife and not a widow, Mary Magdalen remained marginality itself, and the more disturbing, by reason of all the sins to which she had for so long succumbed: *peccatrix, meretrix*. It was rather to men that the preachers spoke of Mary Magdalen, in order to shake them out of their torpor and make them blush for their weaknesses. See what a woman, with her courage and her constancy, was able to do. And you? The power of the exhortation lay, in fact, in a fundamental misogyny. In these homilies, Mary Magdalen is essentially anti-woman. But she is more womanly than the rest, for her sins and her attractions.

These attractions, these weapons with which Satan had endowed women so that they could lead men astray, were made perilously obvious, without it being realized, in the model sermons based on the texts concerning Mary Magdalen. One of them, probably the work of Stephen Langton, is oddly based on a round, one of those tunes meant to be danced to that were sung in Paris and which, as was the fashion, deplored the lot of the unhappy wife. The unfortunate wife, in this case, was Mary Magdalen, and her husbands were the devils of the seven deadly sins who had seized her in turn, each worse than the one before. The last of them, of course, was that of lust, and the woman he manipulated and exploited was a prostitute, thus bewitching and got up to seduce. She was like the 'women of our day' evoked by another preacher, William of Auvergne, proud of their bodies, adorning them 'from head to toe', employing every artifice, make-up and perfume, 'lascivious ornaments, capable of leading into temptation the men walking past'. They employed in particular, as all the sermons said, their long hair, freed from the wimple: 'women's most precious possession', according to Eudes of Châteauroux.

Hair let down and the smell of perfume: both were closely associated in the chivalric mind with the pleasures of bed. To evoke these traps of sensuality was to fan the flames, in the minds of the men who listened, of the fantasies provoked by reading about the eremitical life: the tenderness of a woman's body, naked among the hard rocks, the flesh half-glimpsed beneath the flowing hair, flesh that was bruised but nevertheless glowing, and tempting. Since the end of the twelfth century, painters and sculptors have struggled to give Mary Magdalen this ambiguous and disturbing image. They have not stopped trying, even the most austere of them, even Georges de La Tour, right up to Cézanne.

3

Héloïse

Of all the women who lived in twelfth-century France, it is Héloïse whose memory has remained most vivid. What do we know about her? In actual fact, very little. Meticulous research in the archives has enabled us to locate her among the high aristocracy of the Île-de-France. Descended through her father from the Montmorency and the counts of Beaumont, and through her mother from the *vidames* of Chartres, she belonged, as did Abelard, to one of the two clans that were vying for power in the entourage of King Louis VI at the beginning of the twelfth century. We know that in 1129 she was prioress of the nunnery of Argenteuil, an important position which she owed to her high birth. At that date, the community was dissolved and the nuns dispersed. Héloïse led one group into Champagne, close to a hermitage which Abelard had founded and dedicated to the Paraclete, the Holy Ghost as Comforter. She became abbess of the new community. Abelard, concerned for the welfare of these nuns, composed hymns and sermons for their use, one of which, about St Susan, is a eulogy to chastity. There also survive the forty-two questions that Héloïse put to Abelard. The last of them, and the only one not to deal with the difficulties of the scriptural texts, asks 'if someone can sin by doing what is permitted and even ordained by God'. Abelard replied with a little treatise on marriage, conjugal morality and the need to repress desire and pleasure.

The most substantial, and also the most reliable, information we have about this woman comes in a letter written in 1142. Three persons are involved. One is Héloïse, who had just turned forty, that is, by the criteria of the age, she had entered the ranks of the elderly. The other two are men, both called Peter. One was the abbot of Cluny, head of a vast congregation which extended throughout the whole of Europe and which incarnated the most magnificent conception of monasticism; he was respected and venerated; his moral authority equalled, perhaps even exceeded, that of the pope. The other was Master Abelard, who was the boldest scholar of his day. He had just died, aged sixty-three, in a dependency of the abbey of Cluny where he had been received by Abbot Peter the Venerable.

The letter was addressed to Héloïse and its author was the abbot of Cluny; he was a famous writer, who loved to play with words and phrases. It was an activity at which he excelled. He employed all his skill and his total mastery of the rules of rhetoric to polish this epistle, a letter of condolence and consolation, one of many such composed in twelfth-century monasteries. Such words, dispatched from one cloister to another, such messages, their terms carefully weighed, read and reread by the recipient, not in private but aloud, before the members of the spiritual family amongst whom their life of prayer and penance was led, and such writings, the most elegant of which were recopied, circulated and, as in this case, later gathered into collections, were the means by which a close intercourse of hearts and minds was established between monks and nuns, men and women who had shut themselves away from the turbulence of the world, and who believed that, by this renunciation, they were elevating themselves to the summit of the hierarchy of human values. This type of epistolary exchange encouraged what was probably most vigorous and most original, and was certainly most revealing of mental behaviour and attitudes, in the Latin literature of the period.

Through the intermediary of the count of Champagne,

Peter had just received a letter, in fact an anxious appeal, from Héloïse. To comfort her, he described the last months in the life of Abelard. It had been an exemplary and an edifying life. A perfect monk, absolved, cleansed of all his faults, he had died a good death. It is not Abelard who is of interest to us here, however, but Héloïse. Concerning her, this document, whose authenticity is beyond doubt, provides two precious pieces of information. It states, first, that Abelard 'was hers', that he belonged to Héloïse; in fact, she was bound to him, said Peter, without explicitly referring to marriage, by 'the carnal act', and this bond had subsequently been strengthened by divine love; 'with him, and under him', she had long served the Lord; God now, 'in place of' and 'like another' Héloïse, 'cherished him in his bosom'; he was keeping him for her in order to return him to her at the Last Judgement. Second, the letter begins with a long eulogy to Héloïse. It presents her as a model abbess, the good captain of a little company of women fighting ceaselessly against the devil, 'the ancient and perfidious enemy of woman'. Héloïse had long ago trampled this serpent underfoot; she would now crush its head. Her ardour in battle, which made her a new Penthesilea, queen of the Amazons, the equal of the strong women spoken of in the Old Testament, was owed above all to her intellectual qualities. From her earliest childhood, she had astonished everyone; scorning pleasure, she had thought only of her studies; she had pursued them to such good effect that, in the intellectual domain, she, a woman, had eventually – wonders never cease! – 'surpassed most men'. Entering religion, she had changed not only her life, but all her ideas. She had placed them, in total submission, in the service of Christ, thereby becoming truly 'a female philosopher'. It was this that was the source of her strength.

This is a surprising picture, which it is difficult to reconcile with all that the name of Héloïse now evokes. An image of this woman has become deeply rooted in the European mind, and it is not that of the exemplary nun celebrated by Peter of Cluny, and later by Bernard of Clairvaux. Jean de Meung, in Paris, at the end of the thirteenth century, did not sing of the wisdom of Héloïse in the *Roman de la Rose*, but rather of what made her appear 'demented to many people'. Petrarch, in his turn, marvelled at this folly. It moved Rousseau, Diderot and even Voltaire. It inflamed the Romantics; they went to meditate on her grave in the cemetery of Père Lachaise, and one can still see today on the *quais* of the Seine, at the foot of Notre Dame, on the walls of a house built around 1830, an inscription claiming to mark the spot where this young woman supposedly abandoned herself to all the transports of passionate love. She inflamed Rilke, then Roger Vailland, and still inflames many today. Since Jean de Meung, the Héloïse of our dreams has been the champion of free love who refused marriage because it enslaved and transformed into a duty the free gift of bodies, the passionate woman burning with sensuality under her nun's habit, the rebel who stood up to God himself, and the very precocious heroine of women's liberation.

This image, so different from the first, was constructed on the basis of an event that we know about from two other letters, also authentic, or at least very probably authentic; nothing is completely certain with regard to texts of this type, many of which are purple passages, models of good style produced to impress at literary gatherings or composed as examples of fine writing for the benefit of students embarking on their studies in the liberal arts. Both these letters were addressed to Abelard. The first, like that of Peter the Venerable, was meant to console. It was from Fulk, prior of the abbey of Deuil, near Montmorency, also a member of the circle of powerful families to which both Héloïse and Abelard belonged. Abelard had just been castrated. Let him, Fulk writes, swallow his resentment and not seek to avenge himself. Having entered the monastery of St Denis, he was apart from the world. His aggressors, furthermore, had been punished; they, too, had been castrated and, what is more, had their eyes put out, whilst the man behind them had been deprived of his prebend. Above all, however, Abelard should consider what he had gained from this trial. He was now free, he had been liberated and saved. He had been on the road to perdition. Fulk demonstrated this in his description

of the events leading up to the drama. There had been at
first, immense success, with people flocking from all sides to
hear the master, the 'most lucid source of philosophy'. Then,
the fall: the occasion, 'or so they say', was 'love' (we should
understand by this word male lust), 'the love of all women:
it is by the snares of lust that they capture pleasure-loving
men'. Fulk says no more on this subject; he is a monk, and
monks do not talk about such things. He dwells, on the other
hand, on Abelard's pride: 'Endowed with too many gifts . . .
you considered yourself superior to everyone else, even the
scholars who, before you, had devoted themselves to the
acquisition of wisdom'. Pride first; then avarice: in those
days, a teaching post in Paris made a man rich. Finally, lust:
'whatever you could earn by selling your knowledge, you
flung into a bottomless pit, you spent it on making love. You
lost it all to the rapacity of grasping girls.' Now, however,
you are cured, simply by the removal of a 'particle' of your
body. What a blessing! First, if you earn less, you also have
less occasion to spend: no longer afraid for the women in
their family, your friends open wide their doors. And then,
no more temptations, no more fantasies of sodomy, no more
wet dreams. In fact, castration as liberation. According to
the rules of rhetoric, the letter ends in a *planctus*, the lament
for misfortune. All Paris was in mourning, the bishop, his
clergy, the burgesses, but above all the women. 'Need I
describe the weeping of the women? At this news, tears
streamed down their cheeks for your sake, their knight, that
they had lost. It was as if every one of them had lost her
husband (*vir*) or her lover (*amicus*) in battle.'

   The author of the second letter, a piece of invective, was
Roscelin, a master with whom Abelard had once studied in
Touraine. He was replying to Abelard who had, against him,
taken up the defence of Robert of Arbrissel, the visionary
apostle who accepted women in trouble at Fontevraud; this
was the double monastery where, according to the rule
adopted at the Paraclete, the monks, in subversion of every
natural hierarchy, were subordinate to the nuns and under
the authority of the abbess. Roscelin begins, as defender of
the social order, by attacking Master Robert:

I have seen him welcoming women who had fled from their husband, whom their husband demanded back, stubbornly keeping them until their death ... if a wife refuses to do her duty by her husband, if the latter for this reason is obliged to fornicate here and there, the fault is graver for the woman who compels than for the man who acts. The one guilty of adultery is the woman who abandons her man, who is forced to sin.

And even guiltier, obviously, is the man who detains these women. What matters for us, however, is Roscelin's direct attack on his former disciple:

I saw you in Paris as the guest of Canon Fulbert, received into his house, made welcome at his table with honour like a friend or a member of the family. He entrusted to you his niece, for you to teach her, a very good little maid ... Driven by unbridled lust, you taught her not to reason but to make love. This wrongdoing combines several crimes. You are guilty of treachery, of fornication and of having deflowered a virgin.

Even worse, now mutilated, Abelard still sins through women. The abbot of St Denis allows him to teach. But,

what you earn by teaching falsehoods, you take to your whore as a reward for services rendered. You take it yourself, and what you used to give in the past, when you were not impotent, in payment for future pleasure, you give in gratitude, sinning more seriously in paying for past debauchery than in buying new.

We need not dwell on the extravagance of the language. The laws of epistolary eloquence required, in that baroque age, intemperate expression. Let us confine ourselves for the moment to the content of these three letters. We have two famous, indeed, very famous, 'philosophers', carnally joined in physical love: copulation, according to Peter; fornication, according to Roscelin. In any case, they had formed a couple, and this couple had lasted. Both having entered the monastic life, they had progressed together towards salvation, the woman, however, subject to the man, serving God 'under him'. The man, as was right, was always the one who took the initiative. He, from start to finish, was the active partner.

It was the 'love of women', of 'all women', that had been his downfall. Talent, glory, money: he had easily satisfied his desires. In Paris, knowledge was sold and women were bought. The young Abelard, then, was a womanizer. Where does the truth lie? Is this not, on the part of the fundamentalists, a malicious interpretation of that new concern that, at the beginning of the twelfth century, was leading some servants of God, who cared about the souls of women, to cease to keep so distant from them? Robert of Arbrissel and his emulators, whose disciples, it was widely rumoured, slept with the female penitents, were conspicuous examples.

In the case of Abelard, however, the facts are clear, he had seduced Héloïse. This was, in fact, a banal enough event. The exuberant domestic sexuality of this period is well known. In a large household, that of a noble canon, there lived an adolescent girl, the niece of its head, who was unclaimed; hence, up for grabs. In fact, she was not unlike those young girls in chivalric romances, generously offered for the night by their father to the passing hero, in accord with the rules of good hospitality. In this case, however, the master of the house had not consented. He arranged for the seducer to be castrated, probably in 1113, since it was in the following year that the name of Fulbert, instigator of the castration, who, according to Fulk, was punished by the confiscation of his property, disappears for five years from the lists of canons of Notre Dame. It was a minor event. Nevertheless, in the small world of the Parisian schools and the royal court, the affair caused a scandal: a famous scholar emasculated on account of a woman, also a scholar, and also famous. Imagine, for a moment, a similar misfortune befalling Jean-Paul Sartre in the Paris of the 1950s. It was much talked about, and for a long time. This sensational case could be used as the basis for a fine moral story in which some of the questions which preoccupied men of learning in northern

France at the beginning of the twelfth century could be aired: professional problems, problems of the relationship between the intellectual profession and the vanities of the world, pride and greed; above all, sexual problems. These same questions were posed in a group of letters which were gathered together in the abbey of the Paraclete. They purport to have been written around 1132, nineteen years after the unhappy incident. In fact, the oldest of the manuscripts which transmit these famous writings is much later, contemporary with Jean de Meung. An enthusiast, he translated this correspondence from Latin. It has continued to be read and to move generations of readers. Héloïse and Abelard are there. They speak, confronted in a drama; it has four scenes and a finale, and is preceded by a monologue.

I

On the pretext of consoling a friend, Abelard recounts at length, even complacently, his own misfortunes. He was living happily. Suddenly, he says, a double blow struck him in the two sources of his sin of pride: in his mind, the condemnation and destruction of his work; in his flesh, castration. Central to his confession, then, was the event known to us and its consequences. This man, however, is not the skirt-chaser derided by Fulk; he was chaste. But he was also rich, and 'in worldly comforts, the power of the intellect, it is well known, withers, and is easily dissipated among the pleasures of the flesh . . . because I thought myself the only philosopher in the world, I began to slacken the reins of lust, I, who till then had lived chastely.' In Fulbert's house, Héloïse tempted him. 'Not least in looks', but above all, 'superior to all other women in the superabundance of her learning'. She fell into his arms. He took his pleasure, adding: 'If anything new could be invented in love, we did that too.' He was now a slave to pleasure, he had become, as Etienne Gilson remarked, *recréant*, like the Erec of the romance, forgetful of the duties of his position, neglecting his work, 'spending his nights in love-making'. Unmanned by the 'exhausting' woman, he fell, from the full height of his elevated position.

Héloïse became pregnant. He abducted her and took her to Brittany, his native country. There, she gave birth to a son. Her uncle talked of honour and demanded compensation. Abelard agreed to marry her, on condition that the union remained secret. This was agreed; but between men, the woman not consenting. They forced her into it. Soon after the wedding, held in secret, the ashamed husband, worried for his reputation, shut his wife away in the nunnery of Argenteuil. She had been brought up there, and it might be believed in Paris that she was returning freely, as if nothing had happened, without trace of marriage or motherhood, in order to complete her education in the company of young maidens of good birth, her more or less close cousins. The family of Héloïse felt cheated, and took their revenge. Castrated, Abelard became a monk. It was then that he obliged his wife to take the veil and become, like him, a regular. By the time he wrote this autobiography, he had established her at the abbey of the Paraclete. He himself had for four years directed the Breton abbey of St Gildas-de-Rhuys.

II

This long letter came into the hands of Héloïse, who now makes her appearance for the first scene. She, in her turn, wrote, addressing the man she called her 'husband' and her 'lord', in order to complain, forcefully, but with great dignity. After their marriage, which she had not wanted, preferring to remain, as she put it, his 'whore' so that their love would remain free, her love for him had become so wild that, despite herself, at his command, submissive, obeying not God but him, she had eventually agreed to become a nun. Let him now do his duty as a husband. Till now, he had neglected her, her and the little band of women whose shepherd she was, at the Paraclete. It was because he had always thought only of his own pleasure. He could no longer enjoy her, so he no longer cared about her. She, on the other hand, remained a prisoner of love, of true love, of the body and of the heart. She needed him. In the past, he had initiated

her into the techniques of lovemaking. Let him now help her
to come closer to God.

III

Abelard's reply was distant. The second scene is, in compari-
son, lacklustre. The defaulting husband excused himself,
briefly. If he had given no sign of life it was because he knew
how wise his wife was, and because, in any case, God gives
every support to the women who serve him in nunneries.
Héloïse must continue to manage without him. He was
probably going to die before very long; the monks of St
Gildas were thinking of killing him. Abelard asked the nuns
of the Paraclete to pray for his soul until they had to bury
his body. The prayers of women, he said, and there were
very few people at this period who believed this, were worth
as much as those of men.

IV

It was enough for Abelard to reply, and for him to refer to
his possible death, to give rise to the magnificent passion that
makes the fourth letter so beautiful and carries the dramatic
intensity to a peak. The opening sentence – 'To him who is
all for her in Jesus Christ, she who is all for him in Jesus
Christ' – reveals the reorientation that is already becoming
apparent through the effect of grace and submission to
Christ. Above all, however, it reveals the power of love.
Passion shines through every one of these cadenced, bal-
anced, Latin sentences, whose apparent disorder is there to
express the turmoil of the soul. It is at this point that one
exclaims: here is a pure expression of femininity; here, the
historian of women thinks it is at last possible to hear them
speak, to grasp what they really thought eight hundred years
ago, in the privacy of their own heart. Shuddering, Héloïse
cannot bear to think that Abelard might die before her. In
her distress, she can no longer contain herself, she can no
longer stop herself from attacking God. Why had God struck
them down, and after their marriage, which had, after all,

regularized their situation? Why only Abelard? Was it
because of her? For it was, indeed, true what they said, 'that
a man's wife is the meekest instrument of his ruin'. This was
why the marriage was bad and she had been right to refuse
it. She did penance, but it was not for God, it was in
compensation for what Abelard had suffered. He had been
castrated; she had not. A woman could not suffer this fate.
But nor could she be delivered by this means from the
prickings of lust. In her female nature, Héloïse could not
bring herself to repent. She remained obsessed, in the very
midst of her devotions, by the memory of lost pleasures.

V

She had struck home. In the fourth scene, Abelard comes to
life. To signal the sense of his reply, he addressed her as 'the
bride of Christ'. In fact, the whole letter was to turn on
marriage. He had been a bad husband, lustful, chasing after
his wife, taking her by force even in the refectory at Argenteuil, beating her until she succumbed. His punishment, therefore, was deserved. It had been salutary, because it had rid
him of that part of his body which was the 'seat of lust'. Only
Héloïse was now tormented by desire. She should take consolation from this; through what she endured, she would accede
to the glory of martyrdom. In taking the veil, she had become
the wife of the Lord, who was a perfect husband and, even
better, a perfect lover. Abelard was her servant. She now
ruled her earthly husband. She was his 'lady'. And the prayer
he dictated for her to recite daily celebrated conjugality: 'God,
who at the beginning of human creation sanctioned the
supreme grandeur of the sacrament of the marriage bond . . .
you joined us, then parted us when it pleased you.' Finish
what you began, 'and those you once parted in this world,
join to you for ever in Heaven'. This is precisely what, ten
years later, in 1142, Peter of Cluny promised to Héloïse.

VI

The drama brusquely concludes at the beginning of the next
letter, the last from Héloïse. She complies. She will in future

stop her hand from writing the words that come to her lips, impelled by the violent urges that engulf her weak woman's body. She will force herself to keep silent. Under the seal of this silence, she locks up her love, her bitterness and the torments of her desire. Let us move on, she says, to another matter. What she now seeks from her 'master' is that he compile a new rule for the community of the Paraclete. This question occupies the rest of this interminable and, for us, tedious, *Correspondence*.

This fierce demand for liberty, this silence with regard to contrition, and this passionate love worthy of Stendhal: how was it possible for the abbot of Cluny to have composed such a eulogy of Héloïse, notorious rebel? How are we to decide, of the features that he attributes to her and those revealed by the exchange of letters, which were true? How can the historian discover what this woman was really like?

We must, first, be on our guard. This text is suspect. Doubts have been raised about its authenticity since the beginning of the nineteenth century. Scholars have argued, indeed still argue, for and against. Some see it as the work of a forger. Many believe that the letters attributed to Héloïse were written, if not by Abelard himself, at least, like those of the *Portuguese Nun*, by a man. I will not here enter this debate. I note only the strongest argument of those who believe in a more or less total falsification, that is the cohesion of the whole. This collection of letters differs from all those that were composed at the time, in that it arranges the letters as they are arranged in Rousseau's *La Nouvelle Héloïse* or in *Les Liaisons Dangereuses*, that is one responding to the other. It appears, furthermore, that certain letters, from Héloïse and from Abelard, were not retained; someone wished, by a careful choice, to construct a discourse that was condensed and persuasive. Lastly, like that of a treatise, the text of the manuscripts, all from at least a century and a half later than the events, is divided into chapters prefaced by headings. In the sections attributed to Abelard, there are even cross-references to earlier passages. There can be no doubt that what survives is a meticulous literary construction. It reads like a novel, and a novel whose protagonist, we should note, is a man. Admittedly, the female character counts for more here than in the chivalric romances. The main focus of attention, however, is Abelard, as, elsewhere, it is Tristan or Lancelot. One further point: the body of the work contains too many precious and accurate references to the world of the Parisian schools in the reigns of Louis VI and Louis VII for it to be possible that it was forged at a later date from scratch; it must date from the middle of the twelfth century. It remains the case that this material has been edited by someone whose identity we will never know.

Let us accept that it really was Héloïse who wrote her three letters, which personally I doubt. The historian then has to avoid an error which has distorted, and still distorts, all interpretations of this document. One did not, in the twelfth century, write a letter as one did in the time of Leopardi or of Flaubert, or as one writes letters today, if, indeed, they are still written. All those that have been preserved were, as I have said, intended for public consumption, like sermons, or like tragic monologues, and this is why, a moment ago, I spoke of a drama. Like the great courtly songs of the troubadours, they did not reveal confidences. There were no spontaneous outpourings from one person to another. Their authors thought first of demonstrating their virtuosity as writers, playing on the resonance of the words, or the rhythm of the phrases; they displayed their learning, larding the text with quotations. The latter saturate the letters attributed to Héloïse. Bang in the middle of what seemed to be the irrepressible cry of wounded love, we find phrases from St Ambrose, St Augustine and St Paul, which, for the twentieth-century reader, stifle the emotion that had begun to grip us. The impression that this is not an avowal but a display of scholarship is strengthened when we find Héloïse, playing her part perfectly, acting the role of the stubborn sinner as expounded by St Jerome in his diatribe against Jovinian. 'The memory of the vices compels the mind to revel in them and, in a sense, be guilty of them, even when it does not act'; this episode in the drama is entirely constructed on such a proposition. And the artifice becomes patent when we realize that the same sentence has already been quoted in the confession of Abelard, this time with regard to himself, at the beginning of the journey of redemption, when he sets out on the road to salvation, showing the way as a husband should. At this period, lastly, writing conformed to rules which were very precisely codified and taught. Anyone who is ignorant of them risks seriously misunderstanding the meaning of the discourse constructed in this way. For example, the silence that in the last of her letters, the abbess of the Paraclete imposes on herself, the silence that has enraptured those who have taken it as a proud refusal to submit, is, in fact, a rhetorical figure described in the arts of discourse under the name of *praeteritio*. The contemporaries of Abelard regularly employed it in debates about ideas as a way of bringing a discussion to a close.

The thinking of those who prided themselves on their writing was necessarily expressed in these rigid and conventional forms, of a rhetoric with which we are no longer familiar. This is how the words attributed to Héloïse have survived; and these were texts designed to persuade a large audience. If we do not lose sight of this essential point, and if we put aside the now insoluble problem of authenticity, and take the collection for what those who organized it intended it to be, we are left with the indisputable facts that these words were arranged in a monastery and that their purpose was spiritual edification; the true significance of the text then becomes clear and so, by the same title, does the image of Héloïse held by contemporaries, an image that is singularly different from that formed by the Romantics and that many of us still hold today.

It seems clear, first, that the collection was conceived as a memorial, a monument erected, as was customary in monastic establishments, to the memory of the two founders of the Paraclete. In the manner of a saint's life, it described their 'passion': that is what each of them had suffered, the trials that had been inflicted on them, until they had at last been able to triumph and accede, ultimately, to a sort of sanctity. The correspondence is a detailed account of a double and difficult conversion. It shows, in particular, how one has to struggle to deliver oneself from evil, to regret one's faults, and to repent. It affirms, in conformity with the philosophy of Abelard, for whom the fault was not in the act but in the intention, that the most stubborn sins were not those of the body, but those of the spirit, that, in the most rigorous chastity, one nevertheless remained guilty if one could not master one's lust, if one did not drive from one's mind the regret for pleasures rejected.

This text, then, is primarily a moral treatise, edifying in the same way as the lives of saints and the chivalric romances of the age. It taught, by telling a story, how to behave well. The pedagogic intent is affirmed at the outset, in the first sentence of the Confession of Abelard: 'To excite or moderate the human passions, examples (*exempla*) often speak louder than words.' Indeed, the collection of letters was put together as a vast *exemplum* designed primarily to show how a woman was capable of saving her soul, to this end demonstrating, first, that marriage was good, next that it could serve as a model for anyone who wished to establish a proper hierarchical relationship between men and women within a monastery, and lastly what femininity was, with its specific faults and virtues. Let us look more closely at each of these three points.

Woman was weak; she could not escape perdition unaided. A man had to help her. In the absence of a father, a brother or an uncle, she needed a husband. Among other lessons, the *Correspondence* contains a eulogy of marriage. So, we should note, did Abelard's reply to the last of the forty-two 'problems' Héloïse put to him, agreeing in advance, she said, as she presented her questions, 'to submit, *in this too*, to his obedience'. So the question of marriage preoccupied the abbess of the Paraclete. It preoccupied the Church as a whole at that period. It was the time when theologians were still asking whether it was not dangerous to include the institution of marriage among the seven sacraments. The text I have discussed here takes sides in this debate. It aims to demonstrate, by describing a specific case, the salutary virtues

of marriage. It begins its demonstration, however, by point-
ing out that certain marriages are bad. This was initially the
case with that of the two lovers, for three main reasons.
First, because it was celebrated hastily: a simple blessing, at
dawn, before a few relatives and without the presence of the
large and joyous company required by the nuptial rites, since,
so as to avoid incest and bigamy, weddings should be public
affairs. It was also bad because the intentions of the husband
had not been good; Abelard himself admitted that he had
been motivated by lust, by 'the desire to hold onto this
woman, to keep her to himself for ever', fearing that this
delectable body would be snatched away from him, given to
other men, 'either through the machinations of the family or
by the attractions of the flesh'. It was bad, last and by no
means least, because the wife rejected it; the ecclesiastical
authorities firmly proclaimed that the knot of marriage
should be tied by mutual consent. So this marriage, rotten to
its core, could not convey grace as did a sacrament properly
administered. It had not been, as good marriages were, a
remedy for lust. Married, Master Abelard continued to burn
with passion, pursuing Héloïse even into the innermost
recesses of the convent of Argenteuil, breaking all the prohi-
bitions, forcing her to perform with him every imaginable
'dirtiness'. God was justified, therefore, in taking his revenge
'on the married couple rather than on the fornicators', in
waiting for the union to be sealed before striking. It was
much more serious to sully marriage, which was sacred, than
to copulate here and there. It was also right that the man
alone should first be struck down; marriage made him the
guide of and responsible for his wife.

Duly blessed, however, this marriage was nevertheless a
true marriage. And the redemption of the couple took place
within the beneficial context of the matrimonial union. By
this 'sacrament', said Abelard, the 'Lord had already decided
to make us, *both of us*, return to him'. When, castrated,
pruned, 'circumcised in heart and mind', and regenerated by
the monastic life, Abelard awoke to his duties as a husband,
he undertook to take Héloïse with him on his spiritual
journey, to be the intermediary, as a husband ought, between

her and the divine power. Using his power over her, he drew her, submissive, along behind him. The abbess of the Paraclete admitted this in the first of her letters; it was not love of God that impelled her, she was obeying the man she loved. 'I have done everything you asked me to . . . on your orders I at once changed . . . it is you alone who decided.' Also good was what she still asked of the abbot of St Gildas, that he did not cease to rule over her, that he lead her to better things, he who had once initiated her into guilty pleasures. It is remarkable how insistently this text puts Héloïse in the position of submissive wife. From beginning to end of the exchange of letters, she keeps to the position that was proper for women, the only one that gave them any chance of freeing themselves from sin.

Here, the true purpose of this apology for conjugality is revealed. The eulogy of marriage lends support to the proposal to change the rule previously followed at the Paraclete. Let there be no mistake, the part that we no longer read, which is usually omitted from modern editions – the two last letters in which Peter Abelard, having justified the reform, issues Héloïse with the programme for a new style of monastic life – was what mattered most for the men who put this collection together, and explains why the texts were arranged in the way they are. The *Correspondence* replies, in fact, to that other burning question which, at a time of chaotic expansion in which old habits were being swept aside, divided men of prayer: what was to be done about female monasticism? The reply, scattered throughout the body of the work, was based on four arguments. First, it was good that there were women in the monastic profession; letter III recalls that the most marvellous resurrections recorded in the Gospels, beginning with that of Christ, were witnessed by women, which proved that, in the divine plan, women ought to be included in the work of spiritual resurrection. Second, it was healthy for every community of nuns to be, as at Fontevraud, supported by a community of monks; the dangers of such proximity should not be exaggerated; Abelard, defender of Robert of Arbrissel, showed by the example of Jesus and his disciples that it was possible and legitimate for men to live chastely in the company of women. Nevertheless, and this is the third point, the dispositions of the rule actually in use at the Paraclete – and it was that of Fontevraud – broke with the natural order because they placed men under the control of a woman; St Paul had spoken, the man is the master of the woman, because, and this time it was Héloïse, a woman, who spoke, 'by its special nature, the female sex is too weak'. Fourth, the nuns and their leader ought to be under the authority of a man, like a wife under that of her husband. The conjugal model should prevail. The exemplary history of the two founders was there to prove it. Nevertheless, in order to complete this proof, the *Correspondence* includes two further expositions, one on the basic weaknesses of femininity, the other on what love ought to be.

Has it been appreciated to what extent the work whose meaning I am trying to draw out is misogynist? Is it not primarily a discourse on the functional superiority of man, a discourse whose strongest arguments are, very cleverly, put into the mouth of a woman? The weakness of Héloïse, the weakness of women, which makes them dangerous ('O, great and perpetual danger of women', exclaims the wife of Abelard) and means that they must be kept on a tight rein, is first and foremost that weakness of the flesh that inclines them to lust. Awakened to pleasure by her seducer – it is not said, we should note, in these writings, as in Roscelin's letter, that she had been forced, that she had showed herself more modest than the amenable maidens of the romances – the 'young girl' soon became a slave to pleasure. Like Cécile Volanges; stricken, like Cécile, in her innermost being, she let herself be taken captive, from her first experiences, by the ardour of her body, home of those 'goads' which, nineteen years after losing her virginity, the abbess of the Paraclete admitted could never be rooted out. They tormented her still. The memory of 'such sweet pleasures', whose 'attacks are more pressing in that the nature it assails is weak', 'the obscene fantasies' of those pleasures made her shudder still in the middle of her prayers. This confession is all the more striking in that it is put into the mouth of an abbess of great renown who was no longer young. And it was in this demanding sensuality, in which women's bodies were steeped, that lay the danger for men. It led them to their downfall. No sooner had he enjoyed the young girl, than Master Abelard was a prisoner, totally enslaved to pleasure.

He might, perhaps, extricate himself from sin by marriage; but Héloïse refused. For, however fragile, however vulnerable and given over to the burnings of the flesh, women had a second fault: they were naturally intractable, stubbornly resisting the men who showed them the right path. In the debate that introduces this apology for good conjugality, the young Héloïse plays the role of devil's advocate. The violent diatribe against marriage which is ascribed to her in the supposed autobiography of Abelard, in a chapter entitled 'argument of the said maid against marriage', a Stoic argument, supported by quotations from Cicero and Seneca, which the abbess of the Paraclete repeats in Letter IV, is not unrelated, within this complex work, to another debate which fascinated twelfth-century intellectuals: was it permissible for the clergy to marry, or, more precisely, for the masters, for those who commented on the word of God? By taking a wife, did they not fall from the level that was assigned to them in the hierarchy of human estates? Héloïse replied without hesitation: marriage degraded the scholar because it enslaved him to woman, to one woman; for him, the shame (*turpitudo*) was to submit (*subjacere*), to agree to humble himself. We should not forget, however, what it was the dialectical function of this virulent condemnation to emphasize: this stubborn woman, who did not give in, who, having become a nun, and an abbess, still resisted, and went so far as to inveigh against God, was the obstacle, and women in general were impediments, preventing men from fulfilling themselves. Abelard, throughout his journey, dragged Héloïse behind him like a ball and chain. When he responded from afar to her appeal, he was still dragging her after him, since she had still not given in, and the letters have been arranged as they are in the collection so as to follow closely the stages in this difficult surrender.

All the words attributed to Héloïse, her cries of revolt, the regret she expressed for lost pleasures, her demands for liberty, were certainly not regarded as admirable, as we regard them today. In the twelfth century, they were perceived as so many proofs of her sin and of the wickedness of women. They were a way of exalting the merits of the two founders of the Paraclete: of the abbess, because she had finally triumphed over her femininity; of her husband, for the unremitting toil in which he had engaged in order to save his wife from herself. He had achieved this by encouraging in her heart the sublimation of carnal love. The *Correspondence* is, in fact, akin to the meditation of St Bernard on the incarnation, the affirmation through Cistercian mysticism that man was made first of flesh, so must start from the flesh, seize the amorous impulse in its bodily sources, contain it, and patiently guide its course so that it became the driving force behind a spiritual ascent. The *Correspondence* also contains, with regard to a woman's passion, a reflection on good love.

To begin with, that of the two lovers had something of the love that we call courtly. Admittedly, Abelard was a cleric. But the Parisians, as Fulk of Deuil testified, saw him as a 'knight', one of those young bachelors, conquering and devastating, like Lancelot, like the paladins of the romances. He was extremely gifted, he had everything with which to *allicere*, to attract to him and seduce beautiful women. Héloïse revealed the reasons for his success in Letter II: 'Which wife, which young girl, did not desire you when you were absent, or burn for you when you were present!' Because you were handsome, because you were famous, but above all for 'two attractions through which you could captivate the *animus* (the animal part) of any woman, on the one hand, the gift of writing poems, on the other, that of singing them. For that above all, women sighed for love of you.' Abelard appears here as a troubadour. The songs that were hummed in Paris at the beginning of the twelfth century – they prove, incidentally, that to sing of love in the time of William of Aquitaine was not the privilege of Occitania, and that it is probably unwise to attribute to Eleanor and her daughters the introduction of the manners of the love called

courtly to the courts of northern France – these songs
celebrated the *amie*, the woman loved: 'You put the name of
your Héloïse on every lip.'

   This fits the courtly model perfectly, including the progress
of the seduction, the initial exchange of glances, then the
words, the kisses, and, lastly, touching with the hands – with
the exception, however, of the last touch; the poet did not
respect the rule of discretion. This was not, however, the
chief difference, which was that this lover did not, like
Bernard of Ventadour, sing of unsatisfied love. His song did
not cease when he had captured his prey. On the contrary, it
grew louder, and became a song of victory. 'Because most of
your poems sang of our love,' wrote the abbess of the
Paraclete, 'they aroused the jealousy of the women of Paris.'
What did they envy her? She did not beat about the bush:
'sex', the pleasures of bed. This way of loving was a very
obvious departure from courtly manners in that the fervour
continued after the seduction. Abelard might recognize in his
confession that, once the adventure had been discovered, the
mistress dispatched to Brittany to give birth in secret, and
the wife cloistered at Argenteuil, the 'separation of bodies'
made closer the 'joining of souls'. But he soon corrected
himself: the *gaudia*, the joys of the flesh, were all the more
vivid in that they were more rare. At the end of the day, as
Etienne Gilson has said, this story is 'a sordid affair'. It
crudely revealed the truth of the relations between the sexes
among the avant-gardes of Parisian society: the song as
means of seduction, courtesy as a decoration, as a veil, but
inadequately concealing the reality, that is the sexual
appetite.

   If, in this epistolary novel, lust and pleasure did not
diminish once the man had enjoyed the woman he had
pursued, it is because marriage here is not, as in the classical
schema of courtly love, an obstacle preventing pleasure in
love. Here, bodily pleasure did not die with marriage. On the
contrary, it became more ardent. Héloïse admitted that, after
the wedding, her love for him had become wild, and the love
of which she spoke was not only romantic: 'If you kept me
so tightly bound, it was because I was always prey to an

immoderate love.' I find it remarkable to see proclaimed in this edifying text, written well on in the twelfth century, at the time when the figure of Mary Magdalen, loving but penitent, was being used to suppress sexual sin, that the physical attachment of the woman to the man, and the fervour that sustained shared pleasure, could put the finishing touches to the regulatory function of marriage, inasmuch as the conjugal tie strengthened the power of the husband, 'sole possessor . . . of both her body and her soul', over the wife. Married, Héloïse no longer belonged to herself. She had given herself entirely; she expected nothing in return, devoting herself to satisfying, not her own 'voluptuous pleasures' and 'desires', but those of her lord. She was in a state of absolute submission, subjugated, and it is in the light of this declaration that we should interpret another passage in this same Letter IV. If Héloïse asked to be called 'concubine or whore' – she repeated the rude word employed by Roscelin – rather than wife, it was to humiliate herself further. It was also so that, beneath whatever power and dignity there was in the condition of wife, the tenderness and joyous abandonment of the *amie* would remain. What made marriage good, then, was the submission of the wife, but in conjunction with the ardours of the mistress, as long as her love was free and disinterested. This is why the abbess of the Paraclete was justified, in Letter II, in preferring love to marriage, liberty to chains. She wanted good love to be free of all lust.

This is the chief lesson of this spiritual tract: marriage could also be the forge in which *amor*, concupiscence, was transformed and transfigured, to become, while losing nothing of its vigour, *dilectio*, that is purified passion of the soul. Over this alchemy, presided, obviously, the man, the guide and master, here, Abelard, the first to be cured, despite himself, by the trials inflicted on him by the Lord. Again authorized to teach after entering St Denis, he no longer did so for glory and money, but 'for the love of God'. His violent passion for the body of Héloïse underwent a similar transmutation. *Cupiditas*, the desire to take and to enjoy, gradually gave way to *amicitia*, the gift of oneself, freely, generously, disinterestedly – it was this disinterestedness to

which Héloïse aspired – to that mutual reverence, that
fidelity, that abnegation which, in the humanist renaissance
of the twelfth century, men of culture, rereading Cicero and
the Stoics, placed so high in their scale of values. Abelard,
director of conscience, reached this position in Letter V,
responding to her expectation, agreeing to call 'mistress' the
woman who cried out to him that she was his wife. He used
this word in order to persuade her that she was certainly his
wife, but that her lover was now Christ, and that he, the
carnal husband, was now there only to serve her as the good
knight served his lady. He used this word to affirm that they
were united, as Peter the Venerable would say in his letter,
by 'divine charity', and that they were 'now more closely
linked by a love that had become spiritual', finding its
fulfilment in friendship. When the mistress had at last
understood, she laid down her arms. She ceased to utter
those impassioned cries that a twelfth-century reader, we
may be sure, heard as the detestable expression of feminine
falsity and perversity. She kept silent: 'Speak to us, we will
listen.' These words conclude the last letter from the abbess
of the Paraclete. They confirm that she had fallen into line,
that she had managed to castrate herself: 'I deny myself all
pleasure, in order to obey you.' Through the man to whom
she had once given her body, of whom she had become the
wife, and whose *voluntas*, virile virtue, had ended, because
she had continued to love him, and through turning away
from *voluptas*, from that abandonment to pleasure which
made women weak and dangerous, Héloïse was saved. And
Jean Moline was not mistaken, commenting on the *Correspondence* in the fifteenth century, to see her as an allegory
of the sinning soul redeemed by grace when she finally agreed
to humiliate herself.

In this way, approaching this moving text cautiously,
taking pains to read it as it was read by those for whom it
was written, we at last see resolved all the contradictions
between the Héloïse of the *Correspondence* and the Héloïse
that Peter the Venerable set out to comfort. The true Héloïse
is, indeed, the 'wise woman' of the poem by François Villon,
the oh-so-learned woman who, when she wrote – if indeed

the letters are hers – chose as the best way of showing herself tortured by love to declaim verses from Lucan, and the sensitive and sensual woman, whose sensuality was her strength, because it was this conflagration, in the very depths of her feminine nature, that enabled her to pass, as Peter the Venerable said, from profane wisdom to true philosophy, that is to the love of Christ. She thus became a model and a consolation for all those noblewomen who, in agreement with their husband, entered a nunnery late in life, some of whom may have regretted the pleasures they had once been fortunate enough to enjoy in the marriage bed. But she was a model for men, too. Did not her story, like that of Mary Magdalen, teach them, so as to shake them out of their idleness and arrogance, that the excesses of love, repressed by virtue, were capable of making a female body, however weak and steeped in lust, more pure and more rigorous than their own?

4

Iseult

---

enis of Rougemont said it, it has been repeated, and
it is true: twelfth-century Europe discovered love,
profane love as well as mystical love. This happened
neither painlessly nor without good cause. Rapid growth in
every sphere meant that manners were changing fast, and, in
the most refined circles of the nobility, a problem arose with
regard to women, or rather, to be more precise, with regard
to the whole question of love. High society was losing some
of its brutality. A new order was being established. How
much latitude could be allowed to love, to physical love,
without this order being disrupted? How was desire and its
lawful satisfaction to be accommodated?

In one of the most advanced regions of Europe, north-west
France, this problem emerged earlier and with greater
urgency for two reasons. First, because in these provinces,
the familial policy adopted in the aristocratic dynasties – the
care they took to marry off only one son so as to prevent the
patrimony from being fragmented on the occasion of a
succession – deprived the vast majority of adult males of a
legitimate wife. Jealous of those who possessed one, these
men dreamed of receiving a wife of their own, if not of
taking one by force. They impatiently awaited their oppor-
tunity, often for a very long time. William the Marshal, that
model knight, was still unmarried at nearly fifty and most of

his companions remained bachelors all their lives. They prowled around women, longing to get their hands on one. At a time when political structures were gaining in strength, and when princes were striving to domesticate their knights, and keep them peaceably assembled around them at their courts – those great social gatherings teeming with tempting women – such a press of followers, whether impetuous or dissimulating, milling around both married women and maidens, was a disruptive factor that must be contained at all costs. Meanwhile, and this is the second reason, at this very time, the second half of the twelfth century, and in this same part of Europe, the Church was applying itself to the Christianization in depth of the ruling class. Condemning polygamy and incest, it was succeeding in persuading the nobility to share its own conception of marriage. Whereas it imposed strict chastity on the clergy, in the case of the laity it aimed to restrict sexual activity – inevitable since on it depended the survival of the species – to within the confines of a narrow and consecrated conjugality. The contradiction is obvious: marriage was proposed as the only context within which it was permissible to release the sexual urges; marriage was denied to the majority of men. This contradiction fostered in the minds of all men, whether priests or warriors, the conviction that women were dangerous, agents of disorder, and that there was a pressing need to avert this peril by formulating a code of behaviour which would arrange relations between men and women in a better way.

There is ample evidence of different types for such a preoccupation. Among the clearest is that provided by the literature composed for the entertainment of court society, in the language, consequently, which that society could understand, the Romance language, in 'romance'. Designed to be recited, reaching its audience through the intermediary of professional interpreters, this literature was actually pedagogic. It transmitted a morality, the morality that the princely patrons wished to propagate, and to which end they maintained the poets in their households and arranged for the poems to be performed. Almost all of the latter are now lost but, luckily, the most admired of them were transcribed, and

through these few texts we are able to glimpse what the
sophisticated society of the day believed and how it behaved.
For these romances were mirrors reflecting the attitudes of
their audience. They reflected them fairly faithfully because,
like the lives of saints, they were intended to teach how to
behave well whilst they entertained; they therefore ascribed
to their heroes feelings and postures which, admittedly, since
they aimed to make people dream, departed some way from
the ordinary, from the lived reality, but which could not, if
the heroes were to be imitable, appear too dissimilar to it.
They reflected them also because the attitudes of the knights
of the Round Table and those of the women they pursued
for love were, indeed, imitated. The men and the women
who were enthused by this literature tended to copy their
ways of thinking, of feeling and of acting.

Between 1160 and 1180, the most productive of the
workshops of literary creation operated in the courts held by
the king of England, Henry II Plantagenet, principally in
Anjou, in Normandy and in the duchy of Aquitaine, over
which, by right of his wife, Eleanor of Aquitaine, he also
ruled. At the gatherings over which he presided, fashions
were launched. In order to amuse and educate the knights
assembled around him and the young men whose education
in his household he supervised, the poets in his service
developed his views on a subject that affected all these men,
that of the conflictual relations between male lust and its
object, women, well-born women, obviously, ladies. They
treated this theme in a variety of forms, in lyrical outpourings
lauding *fin'amor*, the love we today call courtly, or by
adapting stories borrowed from the classical Latin authors,
celebrating in their fashion the amorous adventures of
Achilles or Aeneas, or even, and this was the newest way, by
working on the 'matter of Britain', that is a body of legends
drawn from Celtic traditions.

Bards from Cornwall or Wales had probably begun to
recite these legends some thirty years earlier, in the entourage
of the grandfather of Henry II, King Henry I, also duke of
Normandy. They had been rapturously received, rather in
the way we today welcome *reggae* or *salsa*, and for the same

reasons: they were different, they told of another world, they were unexpected, they broke with old habits and suggested new ways of looking at life. The most fascinating of these stories told of love, but of a love that was wild, ungovernable and mad. Or rather they told of a mad lust, that mysterious force that drew a man and a woman together, gripped by an insatiable thirst to merge into the body of the other. This was an impulse so violent and so powerful, so resistant to all control, that, like those inexplicable deaths that people then so readily attributed to the intervention of a magical brew, it seemed to erupt randomly, blindly, by the working of a spell. At the centre of these stories, therefore, were the philtre, mixtures, infusions, 'wine mixed with herbs', prepared according to secret recipes exchanged only among women. If it happened that, by chance, one drank this potion, one was from then on its prisoner. No one could defy its power as long as its properties had not worn off. A demonstration of the disastrous consequences of a desire born in this way, and therefore ungovernable, was likely to encourage, in courtly society, salutary reflections on order and disorder and, in particular, on the problems that resulted from a tumultuous sexuality.

By a process of crystallization, the scattered elements of the legend came to coalesce round a single heroic figure, that of a perfect knight, Tristan. This was, we should note, a male figure. For those who first heard it, this story was not, as it is for us, about Tristan and Iseult, but about Tristan alone; the title given to these works by those who first heard them was the 'romance of Tristan'. This is hardly surprising. Chivalric literature was written entirely by men and chiefly for men. All its heroes were men. Women, though indispensable to the working out of the plot, nevertheless had only secondary roles.

The story of the exploits of Tristan, like many of the lives of saints then being written by monks, and like the autobiography of Abelard, begins by evoking the man and the woman whose union had produced the hero and whose destiny prefigures his, then proceeds from the hero's birth until his death. The story is constructed along this straight line. Twice fighting against monstrous adversaries, twice victorious and, by his victory, liberating a people from oppression, twice wounded, Tristan was twice healed by a woman. The back-drop to these marvellous feats is the sea, with Ireland on the horizon, remote, strange, the Wild West of twelfth-century Europe, where it projected its fantasies. It is surely not by chance that, to enthral their audience – those men of war, who had been, at a tender age, brutally wrenched from their mother and from the world of women, who had subsequently lived their life among men, and for whom the feminine had remained since that separation a territory of nostalgia and strangeness – the poets chose to confront Tristan with a woman from a misty country; or that the sea, dangerous, capricious, scene of separations and of journeys, plays such a role in the story. Tristan is at sea, on board the ship which is carrying him to Cornwall, taking Iseult to her future husband King Mark, when he shares with her by mischance the 'love-drink', one of those love-potions that watchful mothers concocted the night before the wedding so that their daughter would be satisfied, at least for a while, in the arms of her husband. Soon, burning with desire, Tristan, still at sea, takes Iseult. He is from then on incapable of renouncing this woman, even when she belongs to another, and despite the special love he naturally feels for the king, his maternal uncle, despite jealous onlookers and all the pitfalls; and when they are discovered, he carries his prey into the forest, there to live out their wild love, their love-making so violent that their bodies, says the poem, were 'abused'. The sea is again present when, Iseult having been restored to Mark, Tristan marries another Iseult, vainly hoping to liberate himself through her from his desire for the first. The latter, the true Iseult, takes to the sea when the wounded Tristan appeals to her to heal him a third time, from death and from his desire. The perfidious sea detains Iseult, and when she is at last able to disembark, Tristan is alive no longer, he has let himself die.

> You are dead for love of me
> I will act as a true lover.
> For you, I too will die.

Iseult dies in her turn, not from desire but from, in the old French, *tendrure*, from 'tenderness'.

The success of the romance was immediate, overwhelming and lasting. From the place where the original legend had been received and then elaborated, that focal point of chivalric culture, the Anglo-Norman court, the wonderful story swept through Europe, starting with Germany, where the Emperor Frederick Barbarossa was attempting to introduce chivalric customs. Around 1230, in France, innumerable sparkling embellishments were added to create an interminable prose *Tristan*. Half a century later, Italy in its turn succumbed to the charm of the love story of Tristan. This charm has retained its power over the centuries and is far from extinguished to-day. The story of Tristan, all are agreed, is solidly entrenched at the very heart of a specifically European mythology.

We need to go back to the sources of this story if we are to appreciate the spontaneous impulses behind it and must therefore turn to the oldest surviving traces: the poems whose emergence was encouraged by Henry Plantagenet in the 1170s, the years when he was attempting to subjugate Ireland; these were also the years when the choir of Notre Dame was being built in Paris, when Benedetto Antelami was carving a Descent from the Cross for the cathedral at Parma and when the Waldensian heresy was spreading, a few years before the birth of Francis of Assisi. Of these poetical works, rhymed in the French dialect spoken on both sides of the Channel in high society, and which, sadly, can no longer be read today, except by trained philologists, we retain only fragments, with the exception of one lay of Marie of France, which elegantly recounts a single episode in the story. Did Beroul and Thomas, authors of the longest fragments, ever recite this tale from beginning to end, as is done in the saga that Brother Robert wrote down on the orders of King Haakon of Norway? In any case, it is remarkable that, of the story they each composed, what survive today are only the most disturbing incidents, those most capable of moving the audience, because they show a man and a woman in thrall to a mad love.

※

With the passage of time, attention has gradually shifted towards the female figure, towards the person of Iseult, who, in Wagner's opera and in the film of Jean Cocteau, has eventually eclipsed that of Tristan, whereas, in what was a 'romance of Tristan', it was on the male figure that attention was primarily focused; we may even wonder whether the audience did not thrill as much, if not more, as it heard the military exploits of this perfect knight described in vivid detail, as when it listened to the poets sing of his raging passion and the tie that bound him inexorably to his mistress. However that may be, I know of no profane literary work dating from the twelfth century in which the woman occupies so large a place in the story, or in which the female character is described with so much discernment, subtlety and, it must be said, delicacy, caressed by the words that the author has chosen. Iseult owes this pre-eminent position to the effects of the philtre. She, too, had drunk from this potion. She had shared it with Tristan, which not only threw her into the hero's arms but – and this is what made the story disconcerting – subjected both of them to desire in an equality which was then denied by a whole value-system that relentlessly subordinated the feminine to the masculine. Doubtless, this equality was claimed by the boldest thinkers of the day for spouses at the moment when, hand in hand, they concluded the matrimonial pact. Indeed, Abelard went so far as to declare that they met in a similar parity after the wedding, each time that they entered, naked, the marriage bed. Iseult was not, it is true, the wife of Tristan. Nevertheless, she was his equal, in contravention of all the proprieties, of all the prescripts and of all social morality, and this is why nowhere else, in all the material to survive from this period, were the questions that preoccupied the nobility with regard to the condition of women posed with more insistence and freedom.

The poets who treated the Tristan theme were anxious to please, in the first place their patron, then their audience. All of them tried, therefore, to present through the person of Iseult an image of women that would be in keeping with the fantasies of the courtly audience. We are safe in assuming that they succeeded in striking the right chords, since otherwise their work would not have survived. These verses, which were recited from memory every time the work was performed, and which were transmitted by word of mouth, stood every chance of being lost. If we are able to read them today, it is because they gave pleasure and because the story they told fascinated those who heard it. It is for this reason that the account of this affair enables us to reconstitute, with less uncertainty than by other means, an image that it is extremely difficult to gain access to, the image of women and of love which prevailed, in the 1170s, in those outposts of social sophistication, the Anglo-Norman courts. And since each of the authors – Thomas, Beroul and the rest – imagined Iseult in their own way, endowing her with certain feelings, a certain style, certain attitudes, and since they also, to show femininity in all its aspects, introduced two secondary female characters – the queen's confidante and the other Iseult, the wife of the hero – women appear in these poems in many guises, so that the historian is even able to distinguish the different ways in which they were then seen by men.

To all of them, young and old, married or bachelors, and to the women of the court too, Iseult presented an exemplary figure of femininity. She was a lady. Indeed, she was a queen. She led her career as a woman royally. She was the daughter of a king, heiress to a kingdom, and her father and mother gave her to another king. In the flower of her youth, she sat enthroned, beside the master, at the centre of the princely court, that point on which all looks, all devotions and all lusts converged. Iseult was beautiful. She was the most beautiful woman 'from here to the Spanish marches'. Her face was radiant: she had clear eyes, shining golden hair and a fresh complexion. The poems celebrated, but did not demonstrate, the elegance of her body. Discreetly, they at no point spelled out its charms. Indeed, when the queen paraded among the knights for the delight of the court, the grace of her body could only be guessed at beneath the splendid finery; this, in contrast, was described at length, and, con-cealing her figure, further enhanced its seductive power. And when Tristan, separated from Iseult, had a statue of her carved, like the images of saints and queens then beginning to appear on the porches of the cathedrals of France, so that, in a sort of sanctuary to courtly love, he could focus on this effigy his devotion to the inaccessible mistress, the description once again stops at the mantle. What was attractive about this body, in any case, was its sturdy build. We should not imagine an Iseult with the slender pliancy we see in Virgins carved in the fourteenth century, or in the elegant ladies mincing through the orchards of the *Très Riches Heures*. She was a rude beauty. The warriors and the hunters who were first dazzled by this imaginary woman liked firmness and solidity. They looked for endurance and strength in their female companions. They wanted women capable of riding interminably and, like Iseult in the poem, of smashing the teeth of a treacherous counsellor with one of those blows that mistresses of households then customarily employed to punish insubordinate maidservants. Iseult was built to give her husband sturdy and spirited future kings. This would be her fulfilment. In a society based on dynastic structures, femininity was fully realized only in maternity. And Iseult was maternal, a trait of character inherited from the Celtic legends. Endowed with a mysterious power, she eased pain, she soothed and she healed, comforting like that mother for whom the adolescent knights still vainly longed in their innermost being, and whose place they would have liked the lady, wife of the lord charged with their education, to fill. There is, of course, no allusion in the narrative to any possible fertility on the part of Iseult. It was out of the question for this to be mentioned. The structure of the plot precluded it, as did public opinion, which longed for the adulterous woman to be afflicted with sterility, both to punish her and to avoid bastardy, the obsessive fear of which haunted the thoughts of all heads of families.

Because she was an adulteress, and because King Mark was not the only one to enjoy her body, Iseult presented the very large number of knights to whom a wife had not been given with an image that was likely to appeal to them, that of the perfect partner in the game of love. Quickly aroused, readily letting herself be led beneath the 'curtain', to the shelter of the bed hangings, she feared, admittedly, the wrath of her man, and trembled, but her love of pleasure prevailed. Braving the danger, avoiding the pitfalls, discreet, she evaded malicious eyes. If she was discovered, she used craft. She knew how to lie. She lied well, playing with words so that she never perjured herself. She mocked the husbands whose mistake was to be jealous and keep too close a watch over their wife. Iseult appealed to all the young adventurers, new Lancelots, who dreamed of surreptitiously enjoying the desirable bodies whose attractions they guessed at under the mantle of the married ladies they were denied; she appealed because of her perversity.

It is at this point that we must be careful not to be led astray as we read this romance, as when we read the letters of Héloïse. Tristan is the hero, and inspired sympathy. But the person of Iseult, whose function in the narrative is to set off the virile virtues, was certainly not as sympathetic to a twelfth-century audience as she is to us. It is not sufficiently remarked that the story has comic elements. Listening to Beroul, the people of the court guffawed. They laughed at the cuckolded king – and behind Mark they saw the features of Louis VII. They laughed at the dirty tricks that were played on him by the two lovers. But I doubt whether they were always on Iseult's side. Many of them, the married men in particular, must have applauded when they heard Brangain, the confidante, revile her mistress, denounce her mad love, her malice and her lust, and reproach King Mark for his culpable indulgence; he ought to have avenged himself, sent the traitress to the stake and at least defended his honour. 'Deceiver', 'whore'; falsity in the service of lust. Iseult the 'snake', the viper. She incarnated the danger that came from women, that evil, that leaven of sin, which was inevitably transmitted by all the daughters of Eve, the part of femininity that was damned. For the companions of Henry Plantagenet, women also represented weakness, an uncontrollable inclination to abandon oneself to pleasure. Tristan thought like them. He did not doubt that Iseult the Fair was happy and ardent in the arms of King Mark, that all she needed was a man. Out of spite, believing that pleasure would be enough to cure him of his desire, Tristan decided

to take a wife himself. He was mistaken, obviously. Far from
diminishing, 'the desire he felt for the queen' deprived him of
all his resources when confronted with the pretty young maid
who, in the marriage bed, waited nervously to be taken; and
who was unable to tolerate the failure, the 'withdrawal', who
raged at her neglect and burned both with shame and with
unsatisfied desire; a desire that was female, more tumultuous
and vindictive.

> The anger of women is to be feared
> . . .
> They measure out their love
> But they do not temper hate

Iseult of the White Hands, frustrated, jealous, a deceiver
as they all were, precipitated the useless husband's death by
a lie. Tristan was killed by his wife, as, at this period, many
men feared they would be, by that disturbing and unsatisfied
woman who nightly shared their bed. The success of the
legend owes much to the way it combined criticism and
apology, and, while exalting in Iseult the charm of furtive
love, nevertheless denounced what was so often harmful in
wives, thus responding to that latent anxiety which haunted
not only husbands but all men when confronted with the
mysteries of female sexuality.

Rich in meanings, however, the story of Tristan, as it was
told in the twelfth century, did not stop there. Exploiting,
like Beroul, the theme of the philtre, it posed the question of
responsibility for a society being sensitized to this problem
by the growth of ecclesiastical preaching and by more
frequent confession. This reciprocal desire, of the man for
the woman and of the woman for the man, was here the
consequence of a poison imbibed in error, involuntarily. In
these circumstances, of what were those who were carried
away by passion guilty, and who could justly condemn them?
Tristan and Iseult knew that they were innocent. They
believed that God loved them and helped them. In the forest,
the hermit confirmed them in this conviction. No one was
responsible for this all-consuming desire. No one was a

sinner. Nor, then, were the knights who chased married
ladies, or the wives who betrayed their lord and master. We
are all slaves to desire and this servitude is oppressive. Tristan
and Iseult were prisoners of their love, of that violent love
that the poet was careful not to call joyous. When, after
three years, the effect of the philtre wore off, it was for them
a relief. They had eventually admitted it; for three years they
'had ruined their youth in evil'. Iseult regretted 'the name of
queen, her fine apparel and all the maids who had once
served her in her chamber'. Tristan regretted chivalry, but
also, because he had a heart, that he had drawn his partner
into 'evil ways'. 'Liberated' from a mad love, as from a
secure prison, they began to breathe.

The men who were enthralled by this story all desired
Iseult. At times, she outraged them. At other times, they
perhaps, in the end, pitied this young girl, who had been
carried away, one day, by the murderer of her uncle, over
the seas to the bed of a man she did not know; they perhaps
pitied this woman, from then on hounded, divided against
herself, shared, as between those two lions she saw in a
dream when drowsy after love, tearing her apart, torn
between two antagonistic forces of equal power, desire and
the law. This Iseult was pitiable, victim of her own passion
and of the passion that her very presence sufficed to ignite
among the men who were constantly close about her, and
some of whom spent the night, in an opportune obscurity, a
few paces from her bed.

Lastly, when, addressing, he said, 'all lovers ... the
thoughtful and those in love, those gripped by envy or desire,
the voluptuous and the perverse', Thomas retold the legend,
he tried to reconcile its lesson with that dispensed by another
literary genre, the courtly song, and make wild love, contracted like a bad fever through absorbing the 'wine mixed
with herbs', harmonize with the love celebrated by the
troubadours. The philtre was for him only a symbol, and
desire ceased to be simply a physical impulse. Thomas
proclaimed that woman was not simply that body one
burned to caress in secret, and that to hold a body was
nothing if one did not also hold the heart. He emphasized,

therefore, in the last part of the poem, the duality of Iseult. Iseult the Fair, she whom Tristan had once possessed on board the ship, was then separated and confiscated; her body was absent, wholly in the power of the husband. In his bed, Tristan had the body of another woman, his wife. She bore the name of Iseult; she was as beautiful as Iseult; she was her double. Tristan desired her. The law of marriage required him to take this offered body. Love prevented him. For love, *fin'amor*, fine love, was not the quest for sexual pleasure or the satisfaction of carnal lust. It was that sublimated desire, transferred in the indissoluble union of two hearts. To the knights and ladies who listened to him, Thomas proposed, in fact, a new religion, that of love; object of a cult – that cult we see Tristan, in the vaulted chamber, render to the statue he had had carved. Iseult, the distant and separated Iseult, to deserve the devotion that she knows is lavished on her by her lover, choses to wear under her gown, next to her skin, like the Christian ascetics, a shirt of iron. Here, this version of the legend teaches that love is enriched by trials, that, like the love of God, it requires renunciations, that by love, a love necessarily anchored in the flesh, man can rise by degrees to ineffable effusions. At the same time, in the Cistercian monasteries, the mystics from whom Dante would later draw inspiration discovered the same thing. Rising to these heights, love, the reciprocal love of the man and the woman, was placed firmly above the law. Mastering the obscure forces of carnal desire, the lovers cease to be prisoners or victims. They cease also to be innocent. They are fully responsible; they accept their passion, towards and against everything, until death. This love, too, was not happy, because it was impossible. It inevitably fell short of its target. But it was nevertheless victorious, in the transcending of self. This is what a great poet claimed in 1173. Have we, since then, got very much further?

5

Juette

In 1172, a young girl called Ivette, or, rather, Juette, lived in Huy. This small town, situated in the modern Belgium, was enjoying an economic boom, and money flowed freely. Juette was thirteen. This was the age at which girls were married. Her father, a tax collector in the locality for the bishop of Liège, was a rich man. He consulted his family and chose a husband for his daughter.

Juette had no say in this arrangement. She did not loom anything like so large in the minds of her contemporaries as Eleanor of Aquitaine or Héloïse. I discuss her here, nevertheless, because the story of her life has been preserved. It was written around 1230 by a monk of Floreffe, a house of the Premonstratensian Order. He was well informed; the abbot of his monastery had just received the last confession of the dying woman, and he himself had been her confidant. He had listened to her talking and he did his best to record faithfully what he had heard. Through him, and through this conscientious biography, teeming with precise detail, we get an echo of the words of a woman. They are altered, admittedly, by their translation from the vernacular into school Latin, by the prejudices of the writer and by the requirements of the hagiographical discourse. They are audible, nevertheless, like those of the 'matron saints' who were beginning to be venerated in certain provinces of Europe at

the turn of the twelfth and thirteenth centuries, at the time
when Christianity was beginning to be feminized. That is
what makes this evidence valuable, and highly localized
though this female life was, it tells us a great deal about how
the men of this period thought about women.

At the centre of the exemplary story that he composed for
the benefit of the brethren of his order and of the faithful for
whose piety they were responsible, the author placed the
account of a vision with which his heroine had been blessed
and which she had revealed to her confessor. One night,
after a long time spent praying and weeping, she had seen
herself before an angry man who was preparing to punish
her for a fault she had committed in the past. In this man,
obviously, she recognized Christ. Nearby, a woman of marvellous grace was seated. In her distress, the guilty Juette had
turned her eyes, bathed in tears, towards her. The Virgin had
then risen and, bowing, persuaded the Judge to pardon and
hand over the penitent, to be from then on her maidservant,
her protégée and her daughter. The image of Our Lady
beside her Son, imploring his mercy, was a very common
one. It was visible everywhere, carved or painted, and
preachers evoked it in their sermons. It is hardly surprising
that it should appear in the ramblings of a tormented soul. It
was, in any case, the key to this torment and it explains
Juette's whole destiny. She felt she had been saved by the
intervention of a woman from a terrible masculine power.
She had at the same time discovered the nature of the
forgotten sin which weighed on her conscience: she had
sometimes wished for the death of her husband.

Juette had just died in an odour of sanctity. But it was
impossible to credit her with the virtue of those champions
of chastity whose exploits were at that period being celebrated, with accounts of how they had fiercely defended
their virginity. Juette had not fled the paternal home to
escape marriage. Nor had she been able to persuade her
husband to refrain from depriving her of her virginity, but to
live alongside her, in marriage, chastely. Docilely, this child
had let herself be given and let herself be taken and, like so

many young virgins exposed at a tender age to the brutalities of sexual intercourse, she had never got over it. For five long years, she had had to endure the conjugal 'yoke', fulfil her obligations with disgust and suffer the burden of pregnancies and the pains of childbirth. In five years she had brought into the world a first child, who had died almost immediately, then a second, then a third; they were boys, alas, males once again, who had to be cared for. This was the common lot of women. Juette had at least one piece of luck: her husband eventually died.

She thought she had escaped. But she remained attractive, her dowry even more so. There were suitors who coveted her. Her family, naturally, proposed to use her once again to conclude a profitable alliance and got ready to hand her over to the highest bidder. This time, however, she resisted, refusing to fall once again into slavery. Her father begged and threatened, but she would not listen. At his wits' end, he turned to his employer, the bishop. The latter obliged the recalcitrant Juette to appear before his court, an imposing all-male assembly of clergymen in surplices and knights in armour. Trembling, she still refused. How could they force her, she said, to take a new husband? She had given herself one, and the best: Christ. This was an unanswerable defence. There existed within the Church a special order, the order of widows. Suspicious of second marriages, the Church honoured women who, weary of marriage, chose to end their days in chastity. The bishop conceded defeat. He gave Juette his blessing. She was free.

Her troubles, however, were not yet over. The state of consecrated widowhood required that one attend church services assiduously and, of course, keep away from men. A mature and seasoned woman, whose ardour had diminished, might abide by the rules without too much difficulty. At the age of eighteen, Juette was more vulnerable. Satan resolved to take advantage of this. He began by putting himself in her path. When she left her house before dawn to go to matins, she saw him appear at street-corners in a variety of forms, all terrifying. By making the sign of the cross, she surmounted this first test. The devil then set to work with the weapon he

usually employed to bring about the downfall of women. A
man, a close relative of their dead father, acted as guardian
to the two orphaned boys; in this capacity, he made frequent
visits to the young widow. He desired her, hesitating for a
while to declare his love for fear of what people would say.
When he at last confessed his passion and launched his
attack, the indignant Juette rebuffed him, lectured him and
in future gave him a wide berth. But one evening, some
cousins invited her to dinner and to stay overnight. The
gallant appeared; he, too, was to be put up for the night. She
trembled. In twelfth-century houses, even the most opulent,
there was no private place where one could take refuge; as
soon as the lights were extinguished, lone women were
exposed to the lusts of men who went on the prowl, groping
their way from one bed to another. The company slept on
the first floor. The prudent Juette made a bed up for herself
on the ground floor and took a woman companion with her.
Anxiously, she kept watch. She could not, without scandal
or without loss of face, seek for help or escape in the street.
How was she to avoid being raped? Spying through a crack
in the ceiling the approach of the abductor, she appealed, as
a last resort, to the Virgin Mary. This was a good move. This
harassed young woman, her head full of fantasies, saw,
descending the staircase, not the man she feared, but the
Mother of God responding to her appeal. The man did not
deserve to see the Immaculate One, but he heard the sound
and retreated sheepishly to his bed. The apparition heralded
the vision I referred to above of a splendid woman interpos-
ing herself as protector between women and male violence.
Satan was once again vanquished.

However, he still had one last means of corrupting her:
not sex this time, but money. Juette had plenty of it and she
entrusted it to merchants for them to invest and make it
multiply. This was wrong. God did not like people to grow
rich by doing nothing on the backs of consumers and through
the profits of trade. To the bourgeoisie of Huy, however, this
was a venial sin. To atone, they said, it was enough to give
alms. This, Juette did, but to excess. Her father, afraid he
would see his grandsons impoverished and deprived of the

rank that was theirs by birth, removed from her the manage-
ment of her property, which, a spendthrift, her head full of
crazy ideas like all women, she was squandering, gradually
denuding her house of everything that could be sold.

Juette was then overcome by a feeling of being inexorably
dirtied. How could she recover her innocence and return to
the happy times of her childhood? How could she once and
for all escape from all the men who abused her and tried to
lead her into wrongdoing, from her father, from her sons,
from the relatives who bemoaned their failure to make her
remarry, from the lecherous canons whose eyes and sometimes hands strayed over the bodies of pious women, from
all the men who continued to hover around her? After five
years of widowhood, she decided to withdraw from the
world.

For a man, this was easy. He could go on a pilgrimage, or
on a crusade, or even enter a monastery; there were plenty of
them, many excellent, like those of the Cistercian order. But
it was different for women; if they took to the road they
were likely to be assaulted before long. Convents of nuns
were still very rare and, to be admitted, one had to be noble.
Luckily, in this region, from the mid-twelfth century, the
prosperous bourgeoisie, hostile to the local clergy who
exploited them but uneasy about their ill-gotten wealth, had
developed new instruments of collective redemption on the
margins of the established Church. By their alms they supported two sorts of expiatory victims: on the one hand, the
recluses, men and, above all, women, who, shut up for life in
a cell, then bore the sins of the town and purged them by the
rigour of their abstinences; on the other, the lepers, also
enclosed, and the good souls who, imitating Jesus, devoted
themselves to their service, thereby amassing the graces
necessary to the salvation of the urban community. There
was a leper-house in the suburbs of Huy and it was there
that Juette, at the age of twenty-three, went in search of
peace and relief from her obsessions. A woman of extremes,
she was not content to care for the sick, but ate from their
dish, drank from their jug, plunged into their bath water and
immersed herself in their fetid discharges, longing, according

to her biographer, to see leprosy waste her body in the hope
that her soul would thereby be purified of all infection. She
neglected her two sons; the elder was placed very young in a
school which prepared him for a monastic life, whilst the
younger, left to his own devices, went to the dogs, caring
only for money and girls. Juette spent ten years in this active
life. Then, still unsatisfied, she decided on a life of contemplation, and transferred from the order of widows to the more
meritorious order of recluses. This transition was effected by
rites at which it was usual for the bishop to officiate. The
episcopal see being vacant, Juette was blessed by a local
Cistercian abbot, who walled up behind her the only door to
a little house adjoining the chapel of the leper-house. She
never again left it. She lived there for thirty-seven years and
they were thirty-seven years of power.

Juette had not renounced well-ordered bourgeois comfort,
and her biographer, anticipating criticism, thought it prudent
to laud the merits of moderation and discretion as against
the excesses of asceticism. What she wanted was solitude. To
give greater protection against external appeals, a maidservant had been walled up with her. This assistant, anxious to
spare Juette all bodily fatigue, posted herself on the ground
floor before the little window. She received the supplicants,
listened, and passed on messages. Her mistress, established
on the first floor, like Charlemagne in his chapel at Aachen,
or like Christ and the Virgin on the tympanums then being
carved on cathedral porches, descended from time to time
from her eyrie. Generally, she held court on high, inaccessible
and all-powerful. She no longer saw any men, except for a
few especially austere monks, Premonstratensians or Cistercians, who occasionally visited her, and the two or three
priests serving the church of the leper-house. The latter
sometimes bothered her. It was rumoured that one of them,
whose closeness to her occasioned some surprise, had fallen
in love with her. Juette blushed at this and quickly made it
known that it was actually one of her followers who had
attracted the attentions of this male. In fact, she had gathered
under her wing a large company of women, a whole court of
virginal young girls, recruited as children, whom she sup-

ported and whom she educated, adopted and treated like the daughters she had never had; she did her best to dissuade them from marriage, desperate to preserve them 'intact', to protect these lambs from the wolves who lay in wait.

Most of all, her followers were eager that she should be recognized as a visionary; she saw what ordinary mortals did not see, and she had done so for many years. Long before she had gone into reclusion, one of her maidservants had surprised her one morning in ecstasy. Once she was enclosed, her visions became more frequent. In fact, she herself spoke little about them and always circumspectly. But the women who approached her told of finding her in a trance, inanimate, then, when she came to herself, agitated, crying out as if in childbirth, sighing, said the pious biographer, showing that he was not without experience, 'like a woman sick with love'; it was as if she was being dragged away from unspeakable delights. It was rumoured that, rapt in this way, transported out of her body, she went to visit the celestial dwellings. One day, she confessed, she had met St John the Evangelist up there. Celebrating mass, breaking the host before her eyes, he had initiated her into the mystery of transubstantiation. But this was the only time that, while on high, she had spoken to a man. It was usually a woman, Our Lady, who welcomed her and who took her in her arms. This fact, one gets the impression, was a source of some embarrassment to the man who, in the hope of getting her admitted to the company of saints, wrote down and related the marvels that had happened to this clairvoyant. He guessed what detractors would say: had this visionary, who, he readily reported, rejected all male ascendancy, not kept too far from the person of Christ? Accordingly, in a long chapter, he set out to show that, since Mary and Jesus were indissolubly joined 'by flesh and bone', to attach oneself to one was inevitably to attach oneself to the other. Furthermore, in the course of her excursions in the beyond, had not this unhappily married woman seen herself, splendidly adorned like a fiancée, led in procession towards the sublime Husband, he who did not violate the body of wives, for a delectable wedding, the only one in which a woman could be fully satisfied?

In any case, all around Liège, the recluse was regarded as
a medium, an amazing intermediary between the visible and
the invisible. This gift was the basis of her power. Like the
great Hildegard of Bingen, who had only recently died and
whose memory remained vivid, she was believed to be
capable of penetrating the secrets of the All-Powerful. Being
a woman, she had not received the education that made it
possible for her to read the text of the Gospels. But she
claimed that she felt quite at home among the hierarchy of
angels who escorted her to the place of her mystic marriage
and could distinguish the specific properties of the gems
scattered over the wedding robe in which they clothed her.
She was soon besieged with questions: Explain to us what
are the three persons in the divine unity. Do you think, when
you are transported to the celestial court, of beseeching
mercy for us, your family and your friends? Cleverly, she
extricated herself. When the Spirit raises me to the heights,
she replied, I feel myself wholly merge into the unknowable,
I lose all sense of earthly things; when I return, I cannot
express in human language what I saw when I was dazzled.

In any case, it was not this intransmissable knowledge of
the mysteries that gave her a power over the people around
her analogous to that exercised today over many of our
contemporaries by soothsayers and astrologers; it was a
more disturbing faculty, that of discovering the secret faults
of others. She told sinners of the punishments that awaited
them. This usurious canon or that bourgeois lady of loose
morals were warned: if they did not mend their ways, they
would be cast into hell; she had seen flames emerging from
the genitals of a fornicating woman. Nothing escaped her. If
a young girl, her pupil, when she approached the Holy Table,
turned her eyes not towards the Eucharist but towards the
handsome priest who was distributing it, she knew. If a
young monk kept under his pillow the scarf he had been
given by a cousin as a pledge of her love, she knew. If one of
the devout women in her entourage went secretly gadding
about, she knew. And as for the priest who refused her the
communion to which she was addicted, she knew also that
he slept with a prostitute. She saw into hearts and that made

her formidable. Soon, those who did not feel altogether pure dared not approach her. They confided in her servant. But, however quietly they whispered, Juette, on high, invisible, lying in wait like a spider in its web, was aware of everything. Who could say, if not what punishment from heaven, at least what scandal in the town her strange clairvoyance would soon provoke?

Juette's power seems to have been most effective in the case of women. She compelled them to do penance and to renounce the pleasures of the body. Once caught, there was no escaping her control. One day, one of the young girls in her entourage ran off with a cleric who had bewitched her. Six months later, by exploiting the network of male and female recluses which extended from town to town, Juette succeeded in tracking the fugitive down, far away, in the city of Metz. The lost sheep returned to the fold. Miraculously protected by the prayers of her patroness, she had not lost her virginity. Throughout her escapade, she had nevertheless shared the bed of her boyfriend. He had respected her. He had never even seen her naked.

Men, however, were much more resistant. Like the bad priest she had unmasked, one of those who slept in the great church of Huy, and who were in the habit of enticing pious female parishioners into their bed at dawn and then, for fear of being denounced, preventing them from confessing, some of the men she reprimanded were temporarily shaken and promised to mend their ways. But they soon returned to their old habits. There was therefore a divide: on the one hand, the women, dragooned, subjugated, consenting, on the other the men, accused, condemned, incorrigible. The bitter battle fought by the recluse against all bodily desires, but above all against lust, against that sin of the flesh which obsessed her, took on the aspect of an increasingly bitter confrontation, a war between the sexes.

Meanwhile, in this region, a movement whose causes are far from clear to historians was getting under way. Within bourgeois society, more fluid than the ancient aristocracy, increasing numbers of women, adolescents, widows and even wives, in search of greater independence, were beginning to come together in communities for self-defence, taking the form of small circles of religious devotion. Juette took advantage of this movement. She channelled it towards the leper hospital. She made the latter, under her strict control, into a sort of citadel of female freedom, and this institution, which attracted a steady flow of alms and was regarded with an uneasy reverence, appeared, with the passage of time, as an increasingly disturbing rival to the official Church. Juette's power thus gradually eroded that of the canons and that of the clergy, in sum, male power. This matron, this queen bee crouched in her cell, ruling a cohort of fanatical virgins with a rod of iron, came eventually to have no more doubts. One night, had not Mary Magdalen herself come and taken her by the hand to lead her to the feet of Christ? Had not Juette, in her turn, heard the reassuring words: 'Your sins are forgiven you because you have loved much'? At her death, the hour and the day of which she knew in advance, she was confident that the Virgin would personally welcome her and establish her among the ladies of her court in Paradise. This woman became a crucial player on the political stage. The monks of the reformed monasteries, the Premonstratensians and the Cistercians, themselves rivals of the urban clergy, realized this. They tried to attract her into their camp and contain her. They also came to her defence.

For she was attacked. Her enemies returned fire, and they had effective weapons at their disposal. First, they could bank on an incredulity that was fairly general among men. There was no reason to take seriously the visions of Juette, what she claimed had been revealed to her in the night as she slept, or all those stories of ecstasy and apparitions. How did they differ from the tall stories that the many charlatans roaming around villages and small towns at that period used to con simple souls, 'little old ladies', peasant women? Free spirits sniggered and, reading the biography, one senses that its author believed he would have great difficulty in convincing them. Furthermore, at the height of the Albigensian Crusade, it was easy to accuse of heresy this woman who, refusing the mediation of the priests, claimed, stuffed full of the host, to be in direct communication with the Holy Spirit.

To vindicate her, and to use her, it was necessary to win recognition of her sanctity. This is what, by telling the story of her life, the monk of Floreffe was trying to do.

He was unsuccessful. Juette did not become, after her death, the object of a cult. For this, it would have been necessary to convince men; but men remained wary. They were well aware that they now had to take account of women. As a result, they were even more suspicious of them. They thought it was right that women should fear hell and that they should be strictly controlled, but it should be by them. And they should not set an example to those rebellious daughters who were nowadays only too ready to reject the young man to whom their father proposed to give them. There were too many recluses. The bishop of Liège refused the request of the followers of Juette who asked to be shut up, like the dead woman had been, in the hope of inheriting her power, that power which had briefly made the town tremble and threatened the social order. Society defended itself. The visionary was forgotten. Power, real power, remained in male hands.

6

Soredamors and Fenice

S oredamors and Fenice are two maidens who fall in love.
They marry, and love, fine love, survives. These two
images of women are, in fact, only one; the first is
simply a sketch, the second fills in the details and sharpens
the colours. *Cligès*, the romance of Chrétien de Troyes in
which these two images appear, is constructed like the lives
of saints and like *Tristan*; the story of the hero is preceded
by that of his parents, which prefigures his. Fenice loves
Cligès, whom she will marry, just as Soredamors, before she
marries Alexander, father of Cligès, loved him.

In the course of the poem's 6,700 verses, the complex,
teeming plot proceeds by sudden leaps and marvels. Its
characters, like the emblematic figures adorning the rooms in
which princes feasted among their friends, are at the very
pinnacle of the earthly hierarchies: Fenice is the daughter of
the emperor of the West, Alexander and Cligès are heirs to
the emperor of the East, and Soredamors is the sister of
Gawain, the best knight in the world. The story, lastly,
unfolds from one end to the other of the then known world,
from Britain, the 'Great Britain' of King Arthur, via Brittany,
the 'Little Britain', and Imperial Germany to Greece, the
Greece of Ovid, whose *Art of Love* Chrétien had adapted,
the imaginary Greece of the *Roman de Troie*, the fascinating
Greece of perfumes, sumptuous silks and every delight, and

Constantinople, dreamed of by the knights of Europe thirty
years before their descendants seized and sacked 'the town
of lights' and helped themselves to its jewels and reliquaries
in the most fabulous pillage known from the Middle Ages. I
will pass over the sections which deal with the art of war,
although the meticulous description of feats of arms takes up
most of the story, and was certainly not the least popular
part with an audience of warriors, *aficionados* of the joust,
the duel and the tournament; and it was equally appreciated
by the young ladies, who are seen to be just as delighted by
splendid blows with the lance and the sword, broken breast-
plates and severed heads, and as anxious as the knights to

> climb to the balconies,
> the battlements and the windows
> to see and to watch
> those about to fight.

Like all the chivalric romances, *Cligès* is part of the literature
of sport. Its main theme, nevertheless, is love, and the
progress of the latter is described with great sensitivity in the
lively, limpid, spring-like writing of Chrétien.

This progress is first traced in the heart of Alexander who,
having gone to the Arthurian court to be instructed in the
chivalric virtues, there meets Soredamors, desires her, and
secures her as a reward for his exploits. Above all, it is traced
in the heart of the two girls, and the story comes to life when
Cligès makes his appearance. In fact, the hero encounters
many more obstacles than his father in the course of his
amorous journey. Alis, Alexander's brother, has displaced
the latter from the throne. He has sworn, however, not to
marry; Cligès, therefore, will succeed him. But a tempting
match emerges, an emperor's daughter, and available: Fenice.
At once, breaking the agreement, Alis sets off in the company
of his nephew to seek the future wife. In the great hall of the
German palace, she is like a vision. In haste, the maid

> . . . arrived
> her head uncovered and her face unveiled
> and the radiance of her beauty

emitted as much light
as would four carbuncles.

It was love at first sight. Fenice and Cligès, it is clear, are made for each other. On a day that was gloomy and overcast, they were so beautiful, so radiant, that the light the pair of them emitted, as if from a bright red sun, lit up the whole palace. How could the love so suddenly kindled in this blaze be allowed to burn freely, how could all that doomed it be overcome? How could this young girl be prevented from falling into the clutches of that other man who, at that very moment, was receiving her from the hands of her father?

By magic and by spells; by charms, the most effective of which were, naturally, Byzantine, and whose secret recipes were known to Thessala, a native of Thessaly, Fenice's nurse. The potion that Thessala concocted and that Cligès administered to Alis on the evening of his wedding meant that the latter took great pleasure in the body of his wife, but in dream only, that he embraced only a phantom and that the bride remained a virgin. But before she could belong to Cligès, on his return from Britain, he, too, armed by Arthur, it was still necessary to undo the tie that bound her. This called for another potion. This one gave Fenice the appearance of a dying woman, soon of one dead. Some doctors suspected a trick, and tormented her body to make her give herself away. She held out. She enters the tomb, leaves it and, reborn like a true phoenix from her alleged ashes, goes away, to the orchard of a dream castle whose entrance is known to no-one, to savour pleasure for more than a year in the arms of her lover. Alis at last dies. The wedding soon follows, crowning perfect love.

Chrétien de Troyes very conspicuously presented his romance as the antithesis of *Tristan*. The image of Fenice is thus an exact opposite of that of Iseult. As soon as she falls in love with Cligès, Fenice, mastering her own desire, protects herself fiercely. I will not, she says, have us remembered like Iseult and Tristan,

of whom such follies are spoken
that I am ashamed to tell it.

I refuse to lead the life that Iseult led, which was demeaning, because she shared her body between two men, giving her heart to only one of them:

> If I love you and you love me
> you will never be called Tristan
> and I will never be Iseult.

To make the contradiction obvious, Chrétien copied some of the structures of *Tristan* for his romance. Both poems include a nephew, the wife of an uncle, passionate love between girls of marriageable age and bachelor knights, and it is at sea that the love of Alexander is revealed. Lastly, philtres again play a role. But, and this is the first difference, the lovers are much younger. Chrétien is specific; Cligès is not yet fifteen. He is only just old enough to marry, as is Fenice, and as was Soredamors. Above all, love here is not the consequence of one of those mixtures that were concocted by women. It is born of looks exchanged: 'She gives him her eyes and takes back his.' It is through the eyes that the arrow that love has shot penetrates, that dart whose feathers are the 'golden tresses', and which is, in fact, the body of the loved one. It is the whole of the body, the forehead, the eyes, the radiant face, the little smiling mouth, the teeth of silver and ivory, what can be glimpsed of the bosom, 'whiter than new-fallen snow', above the clasp holding together the folds of the tunic. As for the rest, how powerful the dart would be if it could be seen wholly uncovered, if it emerged from its quiver, 'from the gown and from the shift'!

> That is the malady which kills me
> it is the dart, it is the ray,

that element which pierces to the heart. The heart had once been tranquil, since 'what the eye does not see, the heart does not grieve over'. It catches fire and begins to suffer. It is wounded, but with a pleasing wound, with that sweet pain and that delicious torment from which no one wishes to be

cured. Defenceless, the heart is taken, captured. What is to
be done? Admit one's love to her or to him the sight of
whom has caused the problem? But, take care! The rules
must not be broken. So there is neither rape nor adultery. An
anti-Tristan, Cligès restrains himself from demanding love
from Fenice as long as he believes her to be the wife of his
uncle. She, as soon as she feels herself fall in love, fights a
valiant battle against herself, preventing herself from wanting
to sleep with this man who has just taken her heart:

> How can he to whom I give my heart
> have my body
> if my father gives me to another
> and if I dare not go against him.
> And when the other is lord of my body
> If he uses it despite me
> it is not right for my body to receive another.

And later, when Cligès proposes to abduct her, she is
adamant in her refusal:

> You shall never have other joy of my body
> than you have now.

Unless, she nevertheless adds, you manage to separate me
from your uncle; love, carried to its carnal conclusion, cannot
be allowed to destroy lawful conjugality. In which case, in
the walled orchard, did Cligès and Fenice really remain
chaste? When 'they embraced and kissed'? What had they
been doing before they were surprised, 'sleeping together
naked'? Was it, in fact, so very serious to err on this point?
What the romance forbids is not making love, but taking the
wife of another, and betraying one's husband. But, Fenice 'is
wrongly called a wife'. She is not a wife; she has not yet
given her body to anyone. The man who thinks himself her
husband has never enjoyed her body except in a dream.
Should a marriage that has not been consummated be
regarded as a true marriage? In any case, she is believed to
be dead; everyone assumes Alis is a widower. Lastly, they

had given each other their heart, and this mutual gift is enough to seal their union. At all events, the real message of the romance is that marriage is the fulfilment of and, as it were, a new phase in love. It concludes with this lesson. Once married, Fenice was not shut away under the protection of eunuchs, as women were in the East, because her husband had no reason to distrust her. He loved his wife as one loves a mistress, she loved him as one should love one's lover, 'and every day their love increased'.

This is not the poem's only lesson, and it is for a stronger reason that I include here the double image of Soredamors and of Fenice. The hero of the 'romance of Cligès', it is true, is a man. Like his father Alexander, he is famous, he acquires glory and friendships by his prowess and his largess, the results of which are described at length. Nevertheless, the course of events is entirely dictated by women. One example, from among the minor characters, is the queen of Britain who is first to discover the budding love between Alexander and Soredamors. She sees them go pale; but they are at sea, and the vessel is tossed by the waves; she is not sure. Soon, however, when, on dry land, she sees them again, side by side,

> . . . it seems clear to her
> by the changes of colour
> which are the results of love.

Now convinced, she decides to join together these young people who have not dared to declare their love for each other. Sitting between them, she reveals that 'of two hearts they have made but one'. She exhorts them not to indulge in unbridled love, passionate and violent, but to 'be honourably joined together in marriage'.

The young man gives his consent, the young girl 'trembling, gives herself to him'. The queen takes them in her arms and 'gives one to the other'. This was the act and these the words which, at that period, were sufficient in themselves to tie the matrimonial knot. It should, however, have been a man, either Gawain, brother of the bride, or King Arthur, official matchmaker for orphaned girls, who officiated at the rite. Divested by a woman of their prerogatives, they were content to approve.

In the second part of the romance, another woman intervenes and in a more decisive manner: Thessala, the duenna, the 'mistress' of Fenice. Like Trotula, the legendary healer, she knows all the remedies. A magician, as all women are, to a degree, she makes philtres, potions and unguents and uses them, as we have seen, to hoax the husband of her protégée and annul the unfortunate marriage. Other women, more than a thousand of them, guided by Thessala, invade the palace, seize the woman feigning death from the doctors and throw the torturers out of the windows:

> Never did ladies do a better piece of work.

Lastly, throughout the slow progress of love, neither Alexander nor Cligès matches up to the woman who had captivated him. It is almost always these very young girls who take the initiative. Soredamors wished to keep her heart safe; it is taken. 'In deep distress', she tries in vain to recover it; defeated, she knows only too well that it is improper for women to make the running in love: 'I will wait until he notices.' Nevertheless, when the object of her affection says not a word, she becomes impatient and dares to accost him, calling him friend; in other words, she is the first to yield. Fenice, too, was first to reveal her passion, but in spite of herself, and despite her reserve. She was watching from afar the duel in which Cligès, her champion, was fighting. She saw him fall and was:

> so overcome
> that she cried 'God help him'
> at the top of her voice

before falling in a swoon. Spurred on, Cligès gathers his resources, and triumphs. When he is setting off for England and comes to take his leave of her, he at last dares to declare himself, though still in cryptic terms. But on his return, it is she who gives him what he desires and what he has forbidden himself to touch before she grants it to him: her body.

> My heart is yours, my body is yours
> . . .
> when my heart went over to you
> it presented and pledged you the body.

Nevertheless, still dictating events, Fenice decrees that Cligès will never have her body as long as she remains in the legitimate power of a husband.

Chrétien de Troyes puts a high value on marriage. He proposes that love should precede it and keep it alive. He asserts that it is forbidden to undermine this fundamental institution. On the other hand, the women he presents control all the threads of the amorous intrigue. Now Chrétien clearly aimed to please his public. He responded to their expectations. We are therefore driven to conclude that those who listened to him visualized in a new way the relationships between men and women. I have fought long and hard against the hypothesis of a promotion of women in the feudal age, since the arguments put forward to support this thesis seemed to me unconvincing, and I have tried, with regard to Héloïse and, in particular, to Eleanor, to demonstrate their weakness. Before the image of the queen and of Thessala, and before that of Soredamors and of Fenice, I give in. These women are unquestionably not lesser beings, deprived of reason, or brood mares that warriors despised and subjected to their pleasure before throwing them on the scrap heap when they reckoned they were worn out. It is undeniable that the poem presents as an example to the 'bachelors', to the young unmarried knights, a way of behaving very different from that which it is customary to attribute to courtly lovers. Of course, the women are destined to fall, conquered by the love and the desire of the man and by their own desire. But men are asked to stop amusing themselves with the women of other men, not to take by force the virgin who attracts them, not to approach her unless sure of her agreement and, if she consents, not to take her except in due form, making the mistress into a wife. It is accepted that *Cligès* was written around 1176. Should we conclude that manners were at that time changing within the high aristocracy of France? Yes, they were changing, and here are some of the reasons which may help to explain this development.

In 1176, knights no longer spent their entire lives polishing up their hauberks, chasing after wild animals, fighting each other or plunging their beaten and bruised bodies into tubs of boiling hot water. Progress in every sphere had slowly civilized them. At the courts of the great princes, where romances and songs were written, and where the civilized forms of the relations between the sexes were being worked out, it appeared increasingly necessary for the warriors to cease, at least for a time, to go on the rampage. The order that was gradually being established in these places where men and women lived, some of the time, together, and that code, or collection of precepts, instituting what was then called courtesy, required these men to exercise self-control, to contain their urges and their lust, no longer brutally to ravage their prey. The prince thus taught the young men gathered around him, through the intermediary of the poets he maintained, to behave correctly in the company of women. This did not fail to put them in something of a predicament: how were they to handle these intimidating and strange creatures? At bottom, it was no bad thing if they feared them, in the way that Cligès feared Fenice. 'To doubt.' 'Who wishes to love must doubt.' It was better to see these young men before them a little foolish and awkward,

> kneeling
> weeping so much that the tears dampened
> their robe and their ermine

than, like Tristan, with one bound joining his mistress, at night, in the bed of his uncle and lord.

The year 1176 was also, in northern France, the time of the true lift-off of the market economy. Money now circulated with increasing speed, no longer in intermittent trickles,

but in large flows which began to penetrate to the very depths
of the countryside. The wealth of the nobility benefited from
this general growth. The agricultural surplus, everything the
lords drew from the mills, the ovens and the winepresses,
and from tithes, all the produce which accumulated in
seigneurial barns and cellars, found an increasingly ready
market. The number of dependent peasant families increased,
and they preferred to pay their rents and services in money.
To join this inflow of cash came the sweeteners that the
princes, at the head of reconstituted states, based on an
efficient fiscality, distributed freely to win the favour of those
who agreed to serve them. As a result, the role of land in the
fortunes of the nobility diminished. Their wealth became
more fluid and more flexible. It was less of a problem to
share the contents of a coffer between the heirs than the
lands inherited from ancestors. This meant that heads of
households took a more relaxed attitude towards the marriage of boys. They were less reluctant to allow younger sons
to found their own households; they bought what was needed
to set them up, digging into their own purses if the money
brought as dowry by the girl they had chosen for them was
not enough. As a result, the number of men of war that the
matrimonial policy of the great families condemned to celi-
bacy was rapidly reduced. The future knights now knew they
had every chance of receiving a wife. This is why amorous
games tended no longer to be played only on the margins of
conjugality. People began to think that the rituals of courtly
love constituted a happy preparation for the matrimonial
union and that the latter was likely to be more solid when
the spouses loved each other like lovers. This led to a
transformation in the way men looked at women. Men saw
them as much less passive, as real partners who had to be
reckoned with and who, even if they were very far from
being seen as equals, at least deserved to be treated, whether
married or unmarried, according to the rules. It was these
rules of civility that the romance was intended to teach,
whilst at the same time it taught girls not to give way to
passion and to respect the laws of marriage.

It should be added that in 1176, under the leadership of

Pope Alexander III and as a consequence of the thinking pursued in the Parisian schools, these laws had taken shape. And Soredamors who, in accord with clerical precepts, engaged herself

> without excepting
> either will, or heart, or body

and who, because the Church taught that the sole aim of marriage should be procreation,

> found herself full
> of seed and grain of man

less than three months after her marriage, and whose grief at the death of her husband, lastly, was such that, 'she could not survive him', offered the perfect example of the behaviour that court society as well as the ecclesiastical authorities now expected of women.

Conclusion

The profiles of the six (or seven) women I have discussed are very different. As soon, however, as the six images are superimposed, there emerge the three main features which, for their male contemporaries, defined the position of women within the world order.

For them, women were primarily objects. Men gave them, took them and discarded them. They counted them among their assets and personal property. They either, to proclaim their own glory, displayed them at their side, pretentiously adorned, like one of the choicest pieces in their treasury, or else they hid them away in the innermost recesses of their residence, or, if it was necessary to take them out, concealed them behind the curtains of a litter, and behind veil and mantle, since it was prudent to hide them from the eyes of other men who might wish to steal them away. Thus there existed an enclosed space reserved to women, but strictly controlled by men. The time of women was similarly regulated by men, who apportioned their lives between three successive stages: girls, necessarily virgins; wives, necessarily submitting to their embrace, since their function was to bring heirs into the world; and widows, necessarily reverting to chastity. In all cases, they were subordinate to men, in conformity with the hierarchies that, according to the divine plan, constituted the structures of the Creation..

Nevertheless, women did not let themselves be dominated so easily, as the men of the twelfth century learned from experience, and that is why they feared them. Fearing them, they regarded them as naturally bad. Women were rebellious, so men believed it was their duty to discipline them, to tame them and to lead them. They felt they were responsible for their conduct. They were obliged, consequently, to punish the faults women were inclined to commit, to kill them if need be, at least to keep them, like Eleanor, securely locked up. Their innate noxiousness must be contained by all means. Men were convinced, in fact, that women carried within them sin and death. One did not know what they were thinking; they were slippery as eels; they lied.

Women were deceitful because they were weak. *Fragilis* – I repeat the word of Héloïse – was the last of the features that characterized the feminine nature. Women were frail, but also tender, and soft. And it is here that a positive element emerges. There was, all the same, in femininity a value, that impulse whose motivating force was in the flesh and which inclined them to love. St Augustine had said so, and we know how greatly, in the twelfth century, the ideas of this Father of the Church influenced those of the educated elite. He said it in the Commentary on Genesis written to combat the Manichaeans (book 2, chapter 11). This is a dazzling gloss; it is all there in a few words, a profound reflection on gender, on the relations between the masculine and the feminine, based on the phrase: *mulier in adjutorium facta. Adjutorium*, a helpmate, Eve as a tool put by God into the hand of Adam. For what purpose? To procreate, not only sons and daughters, but for a spiritual procreation; children were good works. To this end, the man, himself enlightened by divine wisdom, ought to direct (*regere*), and the woman to obey (*obtemperare*); otherwise, the household was turned upside down and was on the road to ruin. This hierarchy, however, was internalized by St Augustine as he meditated on the biblical verse: 'Male and female created he them.' This verse established that, from the beginning, male and female existed together within the human being. When God removed a part of the body of Adam to make that of

Eve, when he thus created the conjugal couple, the model for marriage, appointing the wife to be the obedient helpmate of the husband, he made manifest the structures of the soul. Just as the latter ruled the body, so, within it, the masculine principle, the *virilis ratio*, virile reason, ruled the *pars animalis* by which the soul commanded the body, the *appetitus*, desire. This part was the female part, which, as *adjutorium*, ought to help in the submission. God had shown that there should be within each human being a sort of marriage, the ordained coupling of the male principle and the female principle, the flesh consenting never to oppose desire to the spirit, desire giving way before reason, and the soul ceasing by that fact to be weighed down, dragged downwards by the weight of the carnal. The anthropology based on the reflections of St Augustine invited every man to consider that there existed within him an element of the feminine, that God had put it there to help him to raise himself towards the good, so that the 'appetite', desire, had some good in it when it was properly governed. But, and this was the crucial point, woman, in the Augustinian schema, was not all animality. She retained a portion of reason; pretty small, of course: in her, desire predominated. This was dangerous, but also a strength, the element that made her able to give assistance to her man as was right. Such a capacity for love must be ruled by reason, that is by the virile, or it would go astray. However, when they were properly guided and controlled, the powers of desire with which woman was by nature invested proved capable of supporting, and very effectively, a spiritual ascension.

This is what men gradually discovered during the twelfth century, and it was the leaven which led to a promotion of women. The true promotion of women lay not in the abundance of jewels with which men, as their standard of living improved, adorned them. It did not lie in the appearances of power that men abandoned to them the better to dominate them. It did not lie in the play-acting of the games of courtly love. At a time when Christianity was gradually ceasing to be primarily an affair of rites and external pomp, of gestures and formulas, when it was becoming increasingly

private, the relationship to the divine now conceived as a
loving impulse of the soul, what improved the position of
women was the realization that they could, like Mary
Magdalen or like Héloïse, be held up as an example to men
because they were sometimes stronger than they were. This
power was rooted in the abundance of their animal nature,
in that sensuality that made women readier to catch fire, to
burn with love. Maybe because the obscurity is dissipated,
maybe because information is less hard to come by, it seems
to us that Europe came, in the twelfth century, to rate the
values of love more highly. It realized that a woman who
loved, like Fenice, made a better wife, that a woman could,
like Juette, clear the mysterious paths leading to marriage
with the Spirit. The women of this period remained, certainly, subject to the power of men, who still regarded them
as dangerous and frail. A few of the latter, however, and a
growing number, discovered them as objects and subjects of
love. They looked at them with a less disdainful eye. In this
way, women began imperceptibly to extricate themselves
from the heaviest of the shackles in which they were bound
by masculine power.